SYSTON IN WORLD WAR II

The Home Front in an East Midlands village

**Felicity Austin, Cynthia Brown
and Ray Young**

SYSTON IN WORLD WAR II – The Home Front in an East Midlands village

ISBN: 978-1-910181-32-4

First edition published in September 2016

Published in Great Britain by the Anchor Print Group Ltd

© Syston Local History Group

Syston Local History Group

The group meets in 'The Link' at Syston Methodist Church on the third Monday of the month at 7-30pm with speakers, outings and an annual exhibition in September.

For further details contact:
Chairman: Tim Garner 0116 2609154; email-timgarner@sky.com
Vice-chairman: Ray Young 0116 2609663
email- ray.a.young@googlemail.com
Secretary: Clive Iliffe 0116 2609081; email-csiliffe@sky.com

This is the fifth publication of the Syston Local History Group.

Syston Past, Syston Past 2, Syston Past 3 and Syston Past 4 are all still in print.

SYSTON IN WORLD WAR II
(SYSTON PAST Volume 5)

*Leicester Road (now Melton Road) in the early 1950s, very little changed since before the war.
On the left Wilby Place and Hill's Drapery shop, in the distance the Bell public house, on the right the Savoy
cinema, Herbert's the stonemasons, the Assembly Rooms with telephone box, the Adult School, and the War
Memorial in the distance.*

Cover Illustrations

Front
Frances Level (nee Wilson) and Eva Simpson (nee Sidaway) – two members of the Women's Land Army
based at Syston. The letters on the tank stand for Leicestershire War Agricultural Executive Committee.
(Jim Simpson)

Back
Ernest Payne's Leicestershire Special Constabulary buttonhole badge and medal
Women's Voluntary Service badge
ARP Warden's gate sign
Margaret Hyman's Women's Land Army armband

ACKNOWLEDGEMENTS

This book had its origins in an event in Syston in September 2015, initiated by Felicity Austin, to commemorate the 70th anniversary of the end of World War II. In the course of planning this, Felicity spoke to members of local organisations that had played an important part during the war, including the Women's Institute, the Allotment Society and the Scouts, and to individuals who recalled their own wartime experiences. Among them was Mrs Dot Wilkes, then in her nineties. Her excellent recall of her service with the Scouts and local Civil Defence Services emphasised the importance of collecting these and other memories before the opportunity was lost forever. As more interviews with elderly residents followed, uncovering a wealth of photographs and other material in the process, Syston Local History Group was approached for support in producing a permanent record of life in the village during the war. This was agreed, and Cynthia Brown, a historian and friend of Felicity, was invited to join her and Ray Young, author of several of the Group's previous publications, to work on the book.

We are grateful to the following people who have shared their own or their family memories, photographs and other items with us. Without their generous help this book would have not been possible.

Grace Berrington; David Borderick; Stella Bowman; Joyce Brewerton; Marjorie Clowes; Helen Cunliffe; Vivienne Everitt (nee Garner); Eileen Freer; Dorothy Foulds; Mary Gamble; Sybil Gamble; Michael Hall; Meg Hendry; Margaret Hyman; Anne Kemp; Leicester Mercury and Leicester Mercury Mr Leicester's page; Jane Matthews; Monica Naylor; Joyce Newton; Dennis North; Doreen Payne; Les Pole; Mary Poyner; Joan Quinn; Christine Sanderson; Betty Simpson; J. Smith; Jean Sikes; Harry Talton; Margaret Thompson; Betty and George Toon; Jennifer Turner; Tony Whitehead; Dot Wilkes.

We would also like to thank Valerie Fairbairn for permission to reprint her mother Betty Simpson's memoir; Joy Lambell for permission to quote from her father Geoff Meadows' letters; and the Record Office for Leicestershire, Leicester and Rutland for help in locating sources.

CONTENTS

1 INTRODUCTION – SYSTON BEFORE THE WAR

Syston was much smaller in area on the eve of the Second World War than it is now. To the west it was bounded by the railway line between Leicester and Loughborough, and there was little to the north beyond St Peter's church except the gas works. On the eastern side the 'Avenues' off Melton Road were cul-de-sacs on the edge of the countryside, while the area south of Wanlip Road was still known as New Barkby. Even in 1931, however, Syston had a population of over 4,300, and an unusually high concentration of manufacturing industry. There were several footwear companies, among them Eatough's in Brook Street, John Montague Rice and Son in Broad Street, and H. Garner in Albert Street. The elastic web manufacturers W. Preston and Son of Leicester opened a factory in Broad Street in the early 1930s, around the same time as the Fosse Dye Works were established in Maiden Street. Billetop and Gilpin, mechanical engineers, had premises in Victoria Street, and Wells' iron foundry was in Wellington Street.

Other local firms included King's cardboard box makers in St Peter's Street, Edwards and Son, catgut manufacturers, in Meadow Lane, and Taylor's window blind works in Albert Street. Syston Fibre Boards manufactured leather board for the footwear industry at Syston Mill, and the Tizer soft drinks factory was located in the old foundry on Wanlip Road. The firm of J. Porritt and Son, organ builders, was based at 83 Wanlip Road from 1928 – 1941. The En Tout Cas company on the corner of Wanlip Lane and Leicester Road, which played a crucial role in building and repairing airfields for the RAF during the war, is listed in pre-war directories as 'poultry house and patent tennis court makers and landscape gardeners'.

Financial services were provided by branches of Barclays and the Midland and National Provincial banks. The main Post Office was on High Street, and there was also a branch of the National Deposit (Approved) Friendly Society on Melton Road. Local tradesmen such as builders, painters and

decorators and plumbers were much in evidence, along with ladies' and men's hairdressers and tailors – one of them a 'ladies' tailor'. There were several doctors and two dentists, and nurses attached to the Syston District Nursing Association on Wanlip Road. Sick dogs and cats were catered for by the Canine and Feline Infirmary at Vine Kennels on Chapel Street, owned by Miss Bessie Thornton. Syston also had its own music teacher, Miss Doris Richardson LRAM ARCM, based in 1936 on The Green and in 1941 in Broad Street.

OVALTINE TABLETS
FOR A.R.P. WARDENS
AND CHILDREN IN
AIR RAID SHELTERS

4d. TUBES
AND
1/3d. FLASKS

R. McLAREN TODD
DISPENSING CHEMIST
The Rexall Pharmacy
SYSTON
TELEPHONE SYSTON 86174.

R. McLaren Todd's advertisement from Syston *Parish Magazine*, February 1942

Many occupations in Syston still reflected its agricultural activities. Eight farmers were listed in *Kelly's Directory* in 1936, mainly producing wheat, barley, bean and root crops. There were several nurseries, a dairy, a cattle dealer, forage merchant and saddler, and the Barkby Road 'Trial Grounds' of Harrison's, the seed merchants. The Syston Hunting Stables and Riding School were located on Turn Street. The village was also well provided with pubs - eight in 1936 - and a wide range of shops from grocers and greengrocers to butchers, bakers and fishmongers, the chemist shop of Robert McLaren Todd on Melton Road, and the drugstore and Sub-Post Office run by Joseph Gamble on Leicester Road. Most local shops were small family businesses, but there was also a branch of Goodall's, a 'high-class' provisions store, on The Green, and of the Leicester Co-operative Society and Worthington's Cash Stores in High Street. The main bus service to Leicester was operated by the Midland Red, but other services were provided by local bus proprietors such as Leonard Pole and Sons on Leicester Road. As well as carrying freight, the LMS railway station on the eastern edge of Syston offered easy passenger access to Leicester, Melton Mowbray and further afield.

The village had a lively social and sporting life, based in part on its churches and chapels: the parish church of St Peter and St Paul, the small Anglican mission church of St Aidan on Wanlip Road, the Methodist Church on High Street, the Primitive Methodist chapel on Melton Road, and a Baptist chapel on Leicester Road (now Melton Road). The Salvation Army also had a presence in Syston, and later acquired premises in Wellington Street. Other local organisations at this time included the Syston and Thurmaston Silver Band, the Syston and District Constitutional Club on The Green, Syston Working Men's Club in Brookside, the village cricket and football teams, a bowling club, and the Wreake Angling Club that met at the Bull's Head pub. Dances and other social events were held at the Assembly Rooms on Leicester Road, where the Savoy Cinema was also located.

2 READY AT A MOMENT'S NOTICE – THE EARLY MONTHS OF WAR

Preparations for war began well before it was declared on 3 September 1939. As early as 1924 the Committee of Imperial Defence had set up an Air Raid Precautions (ARP) sub-committee to consider how to protect the country from a future aerial attack. Over the next ten years or so it discussed such issues as the development of new aerial weapons, and whether shelters and gas masks would be needed. As war seemed increasingly likely, a national Air Raid Wardens' Service was created in April 1937, and local wardens were sent for training at the Civilian Anti Gas School in Gloucestershire. The Air Raid Precautions Act became law in January 1938, and was widely publicised. In March that year, for instance, there was an impressive ARP display in a shop window on the corner of De Montfort Street in Leicester.

Once war was declared, the Chief Air Raid Warden in Syston, Mr W.J. Prince, was able to assure the Parish Council that 'everyone is ready to operate at a moment's notice'. The *Leicester Advertiser* reported

on 9 September that First Aid posts were manned 'day and night', and 150 volunteers had already come forward to 'give a hand with the filling of sandbags'. Blackout regulations were introduced on 1 September 1939, requiring all windows and doors to be covered at night with heavy material, cardboard or paint, to prevent any light showing that might aid enemy aircraft. This proved 'very much more difficult than we imagined', the Syston *Parish Magazine* reported in November 1939: 'Most of us have found it very difficult to prevent our light from showing… It managed to escape top, sides and bottom, and, if the fabric was poor, through!'. Four 'subdued red lights' were placed at the corners of the war memorial early in the war 'as a precautionary measure to assist motorists', but the risks of travelling in the dark, and the difficulties of blacking out large buildings like the parish church, did curtail some regular evening activities.

The Harvest Festival went ahead as normal at St Peter's and St Paul's in October 1939, but its

Wartime Parade in The Brookside – in front men and women of the ARP unit, and behind them the AFS on their fire appliance. In the foreground second from the right is Mr W.J. Prince, the Chief Warden.
(Brian Moreton)

usual week-night service was not held. At the Methodist church on High Street, arrangements to black out the building were 'in hand' by the middle of September, to allow evening services to continue 'as far as possible'; but due to the 'difficulties of wartime conditions', its annual sale of work in December 1939 was abandoned in favour of a 'Gift Day'. This raised £59, more than the profits of the previous year's bazaar. The monthly meetings of the New Barkby Women's Institute were moved from evening to 2.30 pm 'owing to the lighting restrictions' until the summer of 1940, when they were held at 7 pm. In December 1939 there is a reference to blackout curtains to be made for the WI Hall in Maiden Street as soon as possible after Christmas, from fabric obtained from The Beehive haberdashery shop in Leicester.

The call-up of young men to the armed forces inevitably had an impact on local organisations, particularly sporting clubs like St Peter's football team, which was disbanded for the season towards the end of October 1939 'due to the lack of players'. The team had finished second in the Mutual League in the previous season; but only eight of the 12 members who had signed on at the start of the current season were still available, and two of them were due to start military service in the near future. The Syston and Thurmaston Prize Band experienced similar difficulties. In March 1940 it decided to continue 'despite the fact that ten of their members are now serving in the forces. It was stated that women had asked to become members of the band… The secretary [Mr P. Hastings] is trying to get boys interested, and is giving them lessons'. In May 1940, however, it agreed to close down 'until times were better' as most of its members were either in the forces or working overtime, leaving only six able to attend practices. Attempts to restart it later were eventually abandoned, and it was not reformed until the summer of 1946.

Air Raid Precautions display in Universal Tyre Service Ltd premises on the corner of London Road and De Montfort Street, Leicester. This photograph is dated March 1938. *(Janet Palmer, daughter of Ken Perkins of UTS)*

3 STAR-LIGHTS, SHELTERS AND 'THAT SMELL' - CIVIL DEFENCE

SYSTON AIR RAID PRECAUTIONS UNIT (ARP)

The Syston ARP unit was led by the Chief Warden, Mr W. J. Prince, who was also appointed Group Warden for four villages round Syston in September 1941. Other Syston wardens included Victor Pearce, Harry Cooper, and Sid Moreton. The ARP headquarters were in the old Baptist Chapel in Chapel Street, which later housed Syston's first County Library. There was a small office just inside the door, and beds upstairs in the gallery for wardens on night duty. Dot Wilkes recalled that female wardens 'slept downstairs on camp beds, possibly left over from World War I'. Regular inspections and demonstrations kept the unit in practice and reassured the public of their competence in the event of attack. One such demonstration in the Adult School grounds in May 1941, attended by Mr Partridge, senior officer of the Leicester North Division, involved wardens from all parts of the Division, and was said to be watched with interest by many members of the public. A fire was made and extinguished, 'high explosive bombs' were dealt with, and 'casualties' were attended to by the wardens and First Aid personnel.

One of the main duties of the air raid wardens was to enforce the black-out. Getting around safely in the dark was difficult, as Mrs P.M. Cross recalled in *Syston as I Remember It* (Leicestershire Libraries and Information Service, 1992): 'One night as my dad put up the blackouts, the siren went and we were taken to the air raid shelter at En Tout Cas, which was just over the railway station. As we were hurrying along, my father had a fall with my small sister on his shoulders, but you had to hurry all the time…'. The 'star-lights' installed in Syston from 1940 were intended to make things safer by throwing some light downwards, but they became a source of conflict in themselves. Part of the issue was the cost in addition to the standard charge made by the power company. This was reported by the *Leicester Advertiser* in October 1940 as 25 shillings (£1.25) per lamp for maintenance and

supply for eight months, and £1 each for fitting the lights, which would stay on until 11 pm.

ARP Headquarters in the old Baptist Chapel in Chapel Street. *(Ray Young)*

The lights were approved by the Home Office, but despite repeated assurances from the Parish Council, it was widely believed that they were visible from the air, and would make Syston a target for enemy bombs – especially when the 'specimen lamp' fitted on the Brook Bridge in October 1940 was said to reflect 'very badly in the water'. Early in 1941 the Council was presented with a petition about the lights signed by 100 residents, but refused to change its decision. The lights were 'definitely invisible from above', Mr Prince assured them: There is much misconception with regard to reflections on wet pavements etc. They may be seen on the ground level, but go upstairs and look out of the window, and you can't see the reflection then. The airmen were not on the ground level'. A 'small minority' remained opposed to the star-lights, and when they were vandalised in August 1942, the Council decided to take 'strong action' by involving the police.

The lamp columns were important in another respect, as they were one of the places where directions to public air raid shelters were posted. There were a number of these shelters in Syston, as well as those built by individual families. Michael Hall remembers walking along the top of the air-raid shelter on Melton Road, opposite Central Avenue - and falling off into a patch of stinging nettles. Jean Sikes recalled a public shelter opposite 8 Sandford Road - although this was 'not there for very long' - and there were others at the En Tout Cas works on Wanlip Road and the top of Mostyn Avenue. The foundations of the latter were uncovered a few years ago when a new house was built as an infill between two others. Dot Wilkes (nee Woodward) also remembered brick air-raid shelters at the tops of the Avenues, 'where they ended at the dog track'. Harry Talton, who was six when the war started, recalled that 'there were air raid shelters erected on Barkby Road, brick built with a concrete roof. One was opposite Albion Street, but nobody used them'. Mary Poyser (nee Payne) and her family used the cellar of their house on The Green as a shelter. Jean Sykes' family would sit under the dining room table, or in the pantry under their stairs – but on the night Coventry was bombed they went round to her uncle in Wellington Street, who had his own shelter in the garden. Margaret Thompson (nee Astill) was taken to the Anderson shelter in their neighbour's garden in Central Avenue when the sirens sounded.

The ARP was also responsible for First Aid in the event of attacks. Dot Wilkes came to live in Syston in 1940 when she was 15, and became a member of the First Aid Party 'as a shy 16 year old'. The following account is adapted with her permission from her memories of World War Two, which were published in *Syston as I Remember It*:

> 'Most of the space in the chapel was taken up by the First Aid Party, with a small room just inside

being designated for the use of the Air Raid Wardens. The First Aid Party was run by Mr Jack Crump. It was organised into Squads who worked a three-shift rota at night as follows: one night on, sleeping at the headquarters; one night on call to report when the siren sounded; then one night off. The siren was on the roof of Eatough's factory at the top on Brook Street. One squad was led by Mr Henry Moore, Syston's Scout Leader. Another squad was all ladies, and included Mrs McLaren Todd Senior (who was in charge of the ladies' squad), Mrs Stuart Maine, Mrs Norah Porter, three of the Watson sisters, Melba Kirt (who became a lifelong friend of mine), and Eileen Horobin..

> 'My memory of entering the chapel for the first time to offer my services… was the sight of Mrs McLaren Todd bending over the billiard table just inside the door and taking a pot shot. Also there was THE SMELL! What the smell was we never discovered: it wasn't drains, but in my experience there has never been a smell like it! There was a small kitchen at the back where we ate our supper on the nights when we were on duty. Supper for our squad was always collected by Frank McPherson and me. We fetched it from Dodwell's Chip Shop on the green in a large saucepan, very late at night. It consisted of all the chips and bits of batter that they had left over at the end of the evening's trade. It all went down very well in the kitchen in spite of THAT SMELL.

> 'Meeting and practice night was on a Thursday. First Aid training was given by Dr MacIntosh, and our ambulance was kept at Shipley's Garage on the Leicester Road, between Wellington Street and Sandford Road. Some of the First Aid Party saw action in Leicester and Coventry [in November 1940], and also on the night that several houses in Queniborough were bombed, 28 August 1940. We had uniforms: navy boiler suits early in the war, and later navy tunics and trousers worn with a red beret. I thought the latter looked very smart, especially when we were on parade, which happened a lot. We had such events as "Wings for Victory" weeks, which were held all over the country to raise money

Auxiliary Fire Service Personnel with the fire pump towed by Sheffield's Garage breakdown truck; front left George Pepper, front right Fred Sketchley and rear right Roland Higgins.
(Leicester Mercury Group)

for the war effort. Also each week ended with a big parade. Ours started from the Manor Hotel on the main road to Leicester just past Humberstone Lane in Thurmaston and ended on Syston "recce", which is now called Central Park. I think it was supposed to be part of our training in endurance! We marched along following a loud-speaker van which churned out Sousa marches to inspire us. Apart from the uniforms we had steel helmets and special gas masks, which were a terrific ego boost among our work mates who all had "common or garden" civilian gas masks. I stayed with the First Aid Squad until I joined the WAAF, which I did as soon as I was old enough to join up in 1942'.

THE AUXILIARY FIRE SERVICE

The Auxiliary Fire Service (AFS) was formed in 1938, and consisted mainly of unpaid part-time volunteers who could be called up to full-time paid service if necessary, including women over the age of 18. Men were required to be on duty every fourth night and women every sixth night. The AFS was originally intended to assist regular local authority fire services, but in August 1941 the two were merged to form the National Fire Service (NFS).

Syston AFS had its headquarters in a large house on Bath Street, although its vehicle was garaged at Eatough's factory on Brook Street. The officer in charge was Roland Higgins, who worked as an accountant in Leicester during the day. Volunteers were trained early in the war, but despite 'repeated applications' to Barrow Rural District Council (RDC) they had no equipment for some time – 'not so much, even, as a hydrant standard or key', the *Leicester Advertiser* reported in November 1939: 'Should there be a fire they would have nothing to put it out with'. Adequate water supplies in the event of serious fires were another concern, and in September 1940 local factory owners contributed £65 towards the cost of damming the brook, to form a secondary supply of water 'in the event of the main being damaged in an air raid'.

Muriel Tyers (nee Adcock) in her AFS uniform.
(Peter Tyers)

The unit included men above the age for military service, and those in reserved occupations, like Ken Sikes who worked at Wells' foundry on Wellington Street. Full-time members of the NFS could be sent wherever they were needed. Jennifer Turner recalls that her father, Thomas Hubbard, joined the AFS just before the war and served with the NFS after being turned down by the RAF:

'His mother was against him joining the Royal Navy because she had lost her other son in the First World War when his ship was torpedoed. Dad was billeted all over England wherever the

action was, including Coventry. He also went to Humberside to fire watch in Hull and Grimsby, and later was posted to the south coast for two years where he helped with damage caused by the V1 bombs'.

Joyce Newton, whose husband was in the Royal Navy, was among the local young women who served in the AFS. She recalled fire watching from the roof of Eatough's factory, alongside her work at the newly built factory of Associated Electrical Industries (AEI) on Melton Road. This was operated by one of AEI's subsidiaries, the British Thomson-Houston Company, to manufacture aircraft magnetos and starter-motors for the war effort, and later became Thorn Lighting.

Stella Bowman also worked at AEI. She had wanted to join the WAAF, but as her father objected strongly to the idea she joined the AFS when she turned 18 in 1942, bringing with her useful experience of operating the switchboard at AEI. She remembers going on duty downstairs at the AFS headquarters with one other girl from 6.30 pm until 11.30, one evening a week. Stella's father met her and accompanied her home to Barkby Road when she finished her shift. They walked in the centre of the road, she recalled, as they seemed less likely to trip over by doing this. Stella also talked of training with the AFS on Sunday mornings with 'proper army drill' in the road outside HQ, and taking part in local parades. She was not trained to operate the pumps and fire fighting equipment, but did participate in training exercises that involved climbing out of upstairs windows and down the ladder.

Some AFS exercises took the form of competitions against other local units. The *Syston and District Times* reported in August 1941 that: 'Syston Auxiliary Fire Service gained first place in the light trailer competition and were also successful in the gas mask competition in connection with the AFS demonstrations staged on Sunday morning in Mr. S. Freckleton's field on the Wanlip Road, Syston'. On this occasion they were competing against groups from Anstey, Birstall, Barrow, Mountsorrel, Rothley, Thurmaston, Quorn and Woodhouse. These events were often reported in local

Frank Souter, plumber, a member of the AFS, on his 1920s Triumph Model R motor cycle in the early 1930s.
(Val Clements)

newspapers, but there is little other information about Syston AFS until November 1944, when the *Leicester Evening Mail* reported a dispute about its vehicle, UT3139, which had been bought by Syston parishioners for about £90. As the threat of serious bombing receded, this had been 'taken to Leicester and stripped, and £5 offered for the remains'. Syston Parish Council described the offer as 'ridiculous', but the NFS Regional Transport Office was unmoved, replying that:

> 'The vehicle seems to have been a free gift to the Rural Council by the Parish Council or original subscribers. It does not appear that there was any legal document imposing any conditions... The handing back of the vehicle to the Parish Council or original subscribers, for them to dispose of for what they could obtain, was purely an act of grace. Similarly, the payment of £5 for UT3139 was purely an act of grace...'.

The offer was eventually raised to £10, but the ending of this particular story cannot be traced. However, some local companies also had their own fire engines

and fire brigades, as Christine Sanderson recalls. As a child she lived on Fosse Way, and her Uncle Lou [Louis] owned Wells' Foundry on Wellington Street. Her father, Jack Sanderson, was part of its fire-fighting force: 'The engine was kept in one of the garages opposite the bungalow. We had a bell box in the hall to call Dad out for fire duty; green braid on his navy uniform rather than red'.

THE NIGHT LEICESTER WAS BOMBED – AIR RAID MEMORIES

Air raid precautions remained in force throughout the war, and the fear of an attack was ever present. Syston itself was not bombed, but a bomb fell on Queniborough in August 1940, damaging several houses and injuring two people. Anne Kemp's father-in-law 'used to tell a little story about the time the Germans dropped a bomb on Queniborough. He said it hit the toilet at the bottom of Stubbie's garden and the **** splashed all over his cabbage patch and that they had the best crop of cabbages that year. They had never tasted better! How true was this? I don't know'.

17

Local people vividly remember the attack on Leicester on the night of 19 – 20 November 1940. Meg Hendry (nee Newing), who was born in Syston in 1932, recalls that:

'My mother worked in Leicester in the evenings, therefore we (my brother and I) were staying with my aunt, who lived on Melton Road (in the house owned by my Grandfather that I had been born in). But Mum didn't come home that night when she normally did. We were worried sick, and she didn't come back until the morning. Apparently she was trying to get home, but an Air Raid Warden stopped her in the street and insisted that she went down into a shelter'.

Doreen Payne lived as a child at the rose nursery off Humberstone Lane in Thurmaston. 'Whilst the bombs were falling on Leicester' she wrote:

'my mother, two brothers and I stood in a passage-way between the bedrooms of our bungalow where we could hear the aircraft overhead, the bombs whistling down and the continual thuds and explosions as the bombs hit the ground. At the end of the passage-way was the front door, and with each thud the letter-box rattled and bungalow vibrated. We were frightened, but my mother did her best to calm us, even though she must have been nearly at her wits end, as she knew Leicester was being bombed and that was where my father was working in the factory [the British United on Belgrave Road]'.

A few days before Leicester was bombed, Coventry suffered extensive damage during a ten hour attack by the Luftwaffe. Les Pole, who was eight when the war started, remembers it well. His father operated his coach business from a large garage at the back of the family house in Leicester Road, on the corner of Wellington Street:

'The night Coventry was bombed Dad was fed up with sirens going all night and he decided we should all (the whole extended family Dad and Mum, Dad's three brothers and families) go off somewhere peaceful in one of the coaches and stay out, sleeping in the coach. We drove out to Twyford and stopped off at the pub there for a drink, then drove to John O' Gaunt where he parked the coach for the night. We looked up at the sky and could see orange sparks in the sky, it was Coventry being bombed. Two days later Mr Hamson [local greengrocer] went to Coventry. I went with him and saw the utter devastation'.

Harry Talton, whose family lived on Barkby Road, also remembers that night: 'We stood in the streets and although it is some distance away we could see the glow in the sky'. Harry's father Reg was born in Syston in 1898 and ran a gentleman's hairdressers for many years, next to 'Masher' Hill's draper's shop and opposite the Savoy Cinema and Assembly Rooms. His grandfather John Talton kept the Bakers Arms, on the corner of Barkby Road and Melton Road, in the inter-war period. 'We used to stand in the road' Harry also recalled: 'and hear the bombers going over. We could tell they were Germans because they desynchronised their engines because they thought we had sound direction finders, which we did not have'.

Dot Wilkes (nee Woodward) in her WAAF uniform.
(Dot Wilkes)

Pole's Coaches in The Brookside, mentioned by Les Pole in his memoir. Coach drivers were classed as a Reserved Occupation because of the importance of moving workers to their factories. *(Ray Young)*

Helen Cunliffe lived in Nottingham with her mother, but spent a lot of time with her grandparents in Sandford Road. She has 'terrible memories of nights in the air raid shelter in Nottingham, but felt much safer in Syston, lying in bed between my grandmother and my aunt'. Even for children who had not experienced an air raid, the sound of aircraft or the sirens themselves was a frightening experience. For Monica Naylor (nee Higgins), her 'greatest fear was when the sirens sounded and the drone of an aeroplane was above. Sometimes in the daytime the aircraft would sound troubled and I was afraid they would crash'. Christine Sanderson also remembers listening to the aircraft flying over, and her father saying, reassuringly, 'that's one of ours'. Jane Matthews (nee Talbott) recalled staying with an aunt near Coventry when she was under the age of five, and 'being afraid of the wailing sound of the siren that was within a few yards of her house. In later years I went into hysterics when I heard the one on Eatough's factory used for the first time by the local fire service'.

HOME GUARD

The Second Anniversary *Home Guard Bulletin* of June 1942 records that the Home Guard came into being when: 'on 14th May, 1940, Mr Anthony Eden, Secretary for War announced the formation of a new force for Home Defence, to be known as "Local Defence Volunteers," and invited every free able-bodied man to come to aid of his country. Affairs in France and Belgium had become grim and were rapidly deteriorating. The response was overwhelming…'.

The Syston area Home Guard when first formed was part of 'A' Company, Leicester District Battalion, LDV, but as of 1 November 1940 became part of 'C' Company, 6th (Quorn) Battalion, Leicestershire Home Guard. At that time the Company strength was 496 men divided into five Platoons: men of Queniborough, Syston and Thurmaston forming No. 9 Platoon, other Platoons being based in various surrounding villages. In 1942 there was some reorganisation and No. 9 Platoon was divided. Syston then formed No. 10 platoon with their headquarters at Kirby House, on the Melton Road in New Barkby.

It was reported in the Autumn 1942 issue of the *Home Guard Bulletin* that 'a Church parade was held on September 3rd, 1942 (the anniversary of the outbreak of war), at the Parish Church. No. 10 platoon, together with the CD Services, WVS, Syston and Thurmaston Army Cadets, Girls' Training Corps, and other organisations assembled at the Railway Hotel car park and No. 10 Platoon headed the parade to the church, this precedence being mildly challenged by certain "Village Fathers"…'.

The men participated in regular night exercises, simulating attacks on surrounding villages, and also undertook weapons training in the sandpit at Thurmaston and at the Rifle Range on the Six Hills.

The Platoon also led a very active social life with darts, cricket matches, smoking concerts, and Platoon dinners at the Masonic Hall. There was even talk of starting a Pig Club which does not appear to have come to anything.

Towards the end of the war in Europe, when invasion seemed less likely, it was announced in October 1944 that the Home Guard would be 'stood down' on 31 December that year.

Other information about the Home Guard in Syston can be found in *Syston Past 4* (Syston Local History Group, 2013).

4 WAR WORK – INDUSTRY, AGRICULTURE AND FUNDRAISING

WAR INDUSTRIES IN SYSTON

During the war many manufacturing companies had to abandon their peacetime production to meet the demand for weapons and other military equipment. Production in others was 'dispersed' to smaller units to reduce the risk of enemy air attacks. They included the British Small Arms (BSA), whose Birmingham factory was bombed by the Luftwaffe in 1940. Its Browning machine gun was manufactured at Wolsey's hosiery factory in Leicester, and four additional factory units were opened in the city to manufacture the Besa machine guns for armoured cars and tanks. As they had done in the First World War, women took over jobs previously done by men who were called into the armed forces. For most of the war the workforce in Syston consisted mainly of women, older men and those in reserved occupations, working long shifts for up to seven days a week at times of peak demand.

One of the Syston companies that made a major contribution to the war effort was Eatough's in Brook Street. According to a *Commemoration Souvenir* - issued by its directors in 1944 'to show their appreciation of the magnificent response which employees of this Company have made in their service in His Majesty's Forces' - the company had had 1,250 employees at the beginning of the war, and a yearly capacity of 3 million pairs of shoes and slippers across its three factories in Syston, Earl Shilton and Burton-on-Trent. As well as outlining the history of the company, the Syston section lists 61 employees - with a portrait of each one - noting that two (B. Bentley and G.H. Willday) had been killed in action, and four (G.R. Chaplin, T.E. Hughes, P.C. Mason and J.W. Smith) were Prisoners of War.

The *Souvenir* also reports that in 1940 there was a decline in the number of employees in a productive capacity, due to employees joining the Services. In 1941 the Burton factory was requisitioned by the government and refitted as an engineering factory for Daimler of Coventry. Around the same time, the Sileby firm of C. Bray Limited was absorbed into Eatough's factory as footwear production was concentrated into fewer units; and in 1942 - 44 the Syston factory was working under Board of Trade Control with a labour staff of about 550 and a licensed production of around 1,000,000 pairs of footwear yearly. During the war period over 600,000 pairs of clogs for industrial and Service requirements were produced, along with tens of thousands of pairs of the standard electrically heated slipper, a component of the electrically heated flying suit.

Another Syston company, En Tout Cas, put its experience in surfacing tennis courts to good use to build runways during the war. The company was founded in 1908 by Claude Brown, who had bought Thurmaston brickworks in 1901. This later became the En Tout Cas works; but by 1908 the business had declined because the local clay that it used was very porous and absorbed too much water. This led him to patent a method of surfacing tennis courts using crushed bricks, which were used to build courts all over the world. The company also carried out landscape gardening and supplied farm buildings, kennels, garden houses, pavilions, seating and ornaments. By the early 1930s En Tout Cas was contracting for public parks, recreation and sports grounds, golf courses, bowling greens, and covered courts for badminton, fives and squash.

The company's Silver Jubilee brochure in 1933 records the construction of an aerodrome for Captain W. Lindsey Everard at Ratcliffe, claiming that 'he has one of the finest, if not the finest, private aerodromes in the country'. Also listed in recent Air Ministry contracts were extensions to airfields at Sutton Bridge in Lincolnshire, and Lee –on- the- Solent. Closer to home, En Tout Cas was also involved in building the civil airfields at Braunstone, Desford and Rearsby – and with this kind of experience, it was well-placed to tender for

EN-TOUT-CAS

WAR PERIOD 1939-1945

No sooner did war begin than En-Tout-Cas turned over completely from the making of Sports Grounds to essential work. This work included either making outright, or extensions or repair work on 202 Aerodromes; the rebuilding (including engines) of 506 Armoured Fighting Vehicles (Daimler 'Scouts'); the making of tens of thousands of Prefabricated Sections of the 'Uni-Seco' type for war factory buildings of all kinds, and, later, the making of tens of thousands of these same units for 6,000 Prefabricated Houses, and at one time we were making prefabricated wall and roof sections for 90 houses **per week**. In addition to the above, we very early on commenced opencast coal mining, and several opencast coal mines were carried through from beginning to end, we eventually reinstating the sites ready for cropping.

★ Contractors to
The Admiralty,
The War Office,
Ministry of Air,
Ministry of Works

★ Contractors to
The Admiralty,
The War Office,
Ministry of Air,
Ministry of Works

★ *Opencast Coal Mining.*

★ *South entrance to En-Tout-Cas Works.*

★ *Armoured Fighting Vehicles (Daimler Scouts) rebuilt and ready to leave*

★ *Aeroplane Factory designed and built for the Percival Aircraft Co.*

★ *At Your Service.*

En Tout Cas – a page from their Forty Year Anniversary booklet showing their wartime activities. January 1st 1949.

further government work during the war. All but essential work was stopped when the war began, the En Tout Cas 40th anniversary brochure reported in 1949. The work that was 'essential' included building or making extensions or repairs to 202 aerodromes; the rebuilding (including engines) of 506 Armoured Fighting Vehicles (Daimler Scouts); the making of tens of thousands of prefabricated sections for war factory buildings of all types; and at one stage making prefabricated walls and roofs for 90 buildings per week. In addition to this they established several open cast mines, the sites of which were eventually restored ready for cropping.

Ray Young's late father Dick joined En Tout Cas as a tractor driver in 1938, and when the war started he was already working on airfield sites. This was considered important enough for him to be granted 'reserved occupation' status. He spent some time at RAF Sutton Bridge in Lincolnshire, and was also sent to RAF Valley in Anglesey, quite early on when it was just a flying field. During the war it was extended several times, and was being used by 1943 as a transatlantic terminal for the American Flying Fortresses and other large aircraft that arrived in Britain to help bomb Germany. After their wedding in 1941, Ray's parents lived in Anglesey, travelling round the island to judge by the family collection of Welsh postcards, and also back home occasionally on Dick's BSA motorcycle.

In mid-1939 En Tout Cas formed a separate company, British Runways Ltd, in conjunction with British Bitumens Ltd. The new company was investigating the use of a mixture of soil and bitumen to create runways, and by the use of a special mixing machine from America it was claimed that four thousand yards of runway could be mixed and laid in a day. Its contracts included work on RAF bases at Syerston, Balderton, Langar and Wymeswold. It continued to work on airfields after the war, but in June 1945 it changed its name to British Runways and General Contractors Ltd. By then government contracts were declining rapidly in number and it was aiming to broaden its base by building houses and factories, constructing sewers, and preparing sites for building.

Another local company involved in war work was Auster Aircraft, known at that time as Taylorcraft. The company was started by A. L. Wykes in 1938 after he flew an American Taylorcraft aeroplane. This so impressed him that he arranged a licence agreement to build the aircraft in this country, initially at the Britannia Works on Melton Road in Thurmaston, beginning in 1939. The first model Plus C was taken by road by Marshall's Transport of Syston to the private airfield of Sir W. Lindsey Everard, which was used by Taylorcraft to reassemble and test fly the Model C Plus aircraft up to the outbreak of the war. When war was declared all private and club flying and the manufacture of civilian aircraft was banned, and in 1940 the company became a Civilian Repair Unit with the repair of 339 Tiger Moths. Later that year the company was asked to undertake repairs to Hawker Hurricanes, and 406 of these were repaired. In 1943 they were replaced by Hawker Typhoons, of which 281 were repaired.

In 1942 the Taylorcraft Model C was modified for use as an Aerial Observation Post to support the Royal Artillery on the battlefront. After extensive trials it went into service as the Taylorcraft-Auster Mk 1. According to a company history, the name Icarus was initially suggested, but as the Ministry of Aviation pointed out, the wings of this mythical figure melted and dropped off when he flew too close to the sun. It preferred Auster, the name given by the Romans to a warm dry south-westerly wind, and this was adopted. Various other Marks were produced during the course of the war, and saw service on most battlefronts. By the end of the war the company had extended its floor space over ten sites in Rearsby, Thurmaston and Mountsorrel, and in a boot and shoe factory in Broad Street in Syston. According to the *Auster Quarterly* (Spring 1975), one other notable achievement during the war - believed to be a first - was the complete assembly of aircraft, including the installation of engines, by female labour alone. Eventually the women were given a production line on one side of the factory, and the men on the other. A healthy rivalry soon sprang up and the women quickly became experts at their job: so much so that by January 1944 the whole of the Thurmaston factory was 'manned' by women, the majority of them local.

Taylorcraft – Tiger Moths under repair at Britannia works, Thurmaston   *(Auster Heritage Group)*

In October 1940 the 6 Ferry Pilot Pool was set up at Ratcliffe airfield, and remained there until the end of the war. Its central location was ideal for the transit of aircraft to the various repair units and RAF airfields over the Midlands area. Some of the aircraft were delivered by Miss Toni Strodl, who was a ferry pilot for the Air Transport Auxiliary (ATA) and lodged for a time with Alice Goodwill in Broad Street. In his book, *Aviation in Leicestershire and Rutland* (Midland Publishing, 2001), Roy Bonser notes that at least one example of every type of aircraft operated by the RAF during the war landed and took off from Ratcliffe airfield; and it has been estimated that about 50,000 ferry flights originated from there. Additional hangers and other buildings were added to cope with the increased number of staff and aircraft needed to cope with the extra work before the ATA closed down in December 1945.

Many people from Syston were also employed at the Royal Ordnance Factory No 10 (Queniborough). According to Dot Wilkes, a lot of the administrative staff were also brought in and found lodgings locally, and there was also imported factory labour, mostly parties of Irish girls. The factory was built in 1941 – 42 on behalf of the Ministry of Supply, and operated by Lever Bothers of Port Sunlight. As a filling depot, it received high explosives which were then mixed and put into bombs and warheads. The factory was located on the Queniborough and Rearsby boundary between the side of the A607 and the railway line, where East Goscote now stands, and from 1944 it was used by the War Department as an Ordnance Depot for stores and spares.

THE WOMEN'S LAND ARMY

Before the war, Britain was heavily dependent on imports of food, amounting to 55 million tons a year or around two thirds of the total consumed – a level impossible to sustain under wartime conditions. Much of the work of maintaining adequate food supplies fell to the Women's Land Army (WLA), and 'Land Girls', in their forest green jerseys and brown corduroy trousers, became a distinctive presence in Syston and the surrounding villages. The WLA was originally established in World War I to replace male agricultural labourers leaving the land

to serve in the armed forces. It was reconstituted in June 1939 when war with Germany seemed increasingly likely, and by September that year, even before war was declared, nearly 9,000 women had volunteered to serve. They included 120 women and girls employed on farms in Leicestershire and Rutland, rising to 2,145 by the end of 1943.

Eatough's factory in Brook Street showing the Auxiliary Fire Service sign and the air raid siren on the roof. *(George Toon)*

Land Girls did a wide variety of work depending on the nature of agriculture in different parts of the country, which was generally much less mechanised and more labour intensive than it later became. This ranged from general farm work to ploughing, planting and harvesting crops, pest destruction, tractor driving, and milking and dairy work. Many small farms still relied on horse power to pull the plough, and milking was commonly done by hand, twice a day for seven days a week. While there were some initial doubts about the women's ability to replace male labourers, these were soon dispelled. In February 1942, when there were over 700 Land Army girls at work Leicestershire and Rutland, Miss

DIG FOR VICTORY   LEAFLET No. 2

ONIONS ★ LEEKS ★ SHALLOTS ★ GARLIC

ONIONS

THE most valuable onions are those that can be stored for use during the winter. When well grown, carefully harvested and properly stored they will keep successfully for six months. But it is important to grow the right varieties for storing.

Varieties for Storing

Good strains of onions for storage are available from seedsmen, but this season, owing to difficulties in obtaining supplies from normal sources, some of the more popular varieties may be scarce, or even unobtainable, and other varieties will have to be substituted.

In the white-fleshed and other mild-flavoured varieties may be included the flat white Spanish types, such as *White Spanish, Rousham Park Hero, Improved Reading, Market Favorite, Banbury, Nuneham Park, Danvers Yellow Flat* and *Ebenezer*, and the Globe types, such as *Up-to-Date* and *Bedfordshire Champion. Ailsa Craig* is also a good large onion of distinct character and very mild flavour, but is not such a good keeper.

Good keeping onions of darker skin colour and stronger flavour will be found in the Brown and Blood Red groups, and among varieties of these that will be found to be satisfactory are *Brown Globe, Magnum Bonum, James's Long Keeping* and *Giant Zittau, Unwin's Reliance, Suttons' Solidity,* and *Carters' Autumn Queen,* and the American varieties *Ohio, Danvers Yellow Globe, Southport Yellow Globe, Southport Red Globe* and *Red Wethersfield.*

How to Grow for Storage

There are three ways : (1) by sowing seed in the open in early spring, (2) by sowing seed under glass in January and transplanting in April, and (3) by sowing in early autumn and transplanting in March. The first method is very popular and can be freely practised almost anywhere ; but where soils are difficult to work, or onion fly is troublesome, the other methods are suitable.

No matter what method is followed, the onion bed must always be carefully prepared. The soil should be dug early (before Christmas) and be liberally manured. Firmness of soil is essential to good growth.

Early sowing is also important, and to ensure this the bed should be prepared as soon as the soil is dry

Elliott, Secretary of the County WLA Committee, reported that: 'It was amazing how well the girls were doing their work. They were very keen and a good type altogether, and there were very few complaints'. As the *Leicester Advertiser* also noted in the summer of 1944, the proficiency badges and certificates awarded to WLA members at a rally at Rearsby were 'gained as the result of examination tests made by practical farmers. The skill of many land girls is such that even hard-headed tillers of the soil have admitted their misgivings have been misplaced and unwarranted'.

Land Girls usually worked at least 48 hours a week in winter and 50 in summer, but hours could be much longer at times such as harvest. Girls working on farms often lived at the farmhouse, saving them a lengthy journey to work, but the accommodation frequently fell short of what they were used to. As Miss Elliott reported in 1942, 'some farms had no bathrooms' and 'some of the girls expected hot baths several times a week.' They were expected to keep their own rooms tidy', but not to do domestic work: something that caused a degree of discontent when farmers' wives struggled to find anyone else to help. He 'could not see it as a hardship if the girls agreed to do some work in the house', one member of the local National Farmers' Union Committee said in 1942: 'though not in the sense of being a domestic servant, of course'. Others were found lodgings near to their farms. Moira Tunnicliffe worked as a Land Girl for Queniborough farmer Jack Stubbs, who grew cereal crops and kept cows, pigs and geese. As there was no room to house her at the farmhouse on Main Street she was lodged with another family member in the village. If no accommodation was available in the farmhouse or neighbouring houses, the girls were equipped with bicycles to get them to and from work.

Hostels for the WLA were also provided as the war continued. The first hostel in the Melton area was opened at Somerby in May 1942, instituted by the YWCA. This was the fifth in the county, and 38 new recruits from Nottingham were 'welcomed to live there' and enjoy its 'comfortably furnished dining room and lounge'. Sometimes large country houses were offered or requisitioned for the purpose, as was the case at Rearsby, but the WLA hostel in Syston

was purpose-built in the autumn of 1943 at the top of Central Avenue, at that time a dead end road on the edge of the countryside. It was a wooden building, with accommodation for about 20 women and girls, including a large dormitory and dining room. The hostel was supervised by a warden, Miss Homefield, and a deputy warden. Mary Lowe, who lived on Millstone Lane, was the cook there, and her teenage daughter Betty sometimes helped her - which is how Betty came make friends with a girl named Dorothy (Dolly) from Sheffield. Girls came from all over the country, as the need for labour dictated, and Betty and Dolly kept in touch for many years after the end of the war.

Other Land Girls were moved to the Syston hostel in December 1944 when the Rearsby hostel was requisitioned for Italian Prisoners of War – despite strong opposition from the girls themselves. They felt 'far from happy at the prospect of Italians living in their hostel and trampling the grounds that the land girls' own work has kept so ordered and neat', the *Leicester Evening Mail* reported, particularly those with relatives killed in the Italian campaign or held as POWs elsewhere. Nevertheless, despite a petition signed by the villagers, 'good luck' messages from US troops stationed nearby, and a half-day strike, they were duly turned out of the hostel, singing popular songs as they left.

Land Girls living in hostels were generally sent where they were needed rather than being attached to a particular farm, but in 1944 a new scheme was introduced as an experiment to allow them to work for individual farmers, 'as there was 'generally more satisfaction when a land girl can stay on one farm instead of being sent to do special work and then leaving after a short time'. Life on a farm or in lodgings could be lonely, and the hostels often offered organised entertainment and education sessions as well as the company of other Land Girls. One such example was the film shown at the Syston hostel in January 1944 on plough setting and 'the finer points of the technique of ploughing'. In October 1943 the Syston Women's Institute also agreed to loan its hall for 'handicraft instruction' for Land Army Girls from a local hostel. The suggested crafts included sandal making and gloving. Land Girls could also apply to stay at Land Army House, the WLA headquarters in Sloane Square in London for a break. Margaret Hyman was among the local Land Girls who took advantage of the opportunity, which required them to take a pair of pyjamas – maybe for a quick and decent exit to an air raid shelter, but she had to borrow some for the purpose as she usually wore a nightgown.

Women's Land Army members seated on the steps of St Paul's Cathedral, Margaret Hyman rear right.
(Margaret Hyman)

Some of the women living in the Syston hostel can be identified from post-war electoral rolls. Among those listed there in October 1945 were Mavis Armitage, Barbara Bryan, Florence Dodd, Betty Goadby, Evelyn Simpkin, Eva Sidaway, and Elizabeth Vann. Mavis Armitage, Eva Sidaway and Evelyn Simpkin were still living there in 1947, while others in that year included Hilda Brotherhood, Marion Chalk, Ruth Glossop, and Jessie and Mavis Lindley. When the hostel was closed later in 1947 the women were relocated to Rearsby House, which by then had reverted to use as a WLA hostel. The Syston building became the local police station until this was moved to The Firs on Melton Road.

There was a continuing need for agricultural labour after the war as the country adjusted to peacetime conditions, and the Women's Land Army itself was not disbanded until 1950. Unlike ex-servicemen and women and those in other auxiliary services, former Land Girls received no gratuity from the government, nor any official help in finding other work once discharged, prompting the resignation of Lady Denman, Director of the WLA, in protest.

Until 2007, when Land Army and Timber Corps Veterans Badges were awarded to surviving members of the WLA, their only official recognition was a certificate thanking them for their 'loyal and devoted' service, signed by Queen Elizabeth, who also commended them at a ceremony in 1950 for their 'courage in responding readily to a call which they knew must bring them… hardship and sometimes loneliness'.

THE WOMEN'S INSTITUTE

At the start of World War II the National Federation of Women's Institutes (NFWI) had more than 5,500 branches and over 320,000 members, making it the largest voluntary non-military organisation in Britain. The local branch was New Barkby WI which owned a small hall on Maiden Street. This was opened in 1934 and still stands, but is now used as business premises. The New Barkby WI records surviving from this time cover the period from 1938, when ARP regulations were coming into force, to the early months of 1944. Although incomplete, they give a very good sense of how the local WI was affected by the war, and how it contributed to the national organisation's war work.

As an established organisation with a strong rural presence, the WI was seen as having a crucial role to play in wartime, although its strong anti-war stance ruled out work directly related to the military aspect of the war. One of its most important activities was food preservation, in which members were already very experienced. There was a glut of fruit in the first autumn of the war, and WIs all over Britain organised jam-making parties to save it from going to waste. The New Barkby Minutes for October 1939 note that 'sugar for preserving purposes was available for Institute members, orders to be sent to the NFWI office, London. 37 members availed themselves of this offer'. Mrs Edna Smith, a young mother whose husband was serving in the army, was one of the New Barkby members who spent whole days preparing the fruit and making hundreds of pots of jam - but as her daughter recalled, this was far from her only contribution to the war effort. Edna was also a member of the WVS in Leicester, and housed an evacuee from Sheffield as well as having a nurse and later a schoolteacher billeted with her.

In 1940 the NFWI was asked by the government to organise a national scheme for making jam and bottling and canning fruit. Sugar was rationed early in the war, but a government grant enabled the NFWI to buy £1,400 worth of sugar that year for distribution through County Federations to branches willing to take part. This Co-operative Fruit Preservation Scheme 'met with a good response' when put to New Barkby members, and the first 4 hundredweight of the 12 requested was received in July 1940. There is no record of the amount of preserves the branch produced, but by the end of the year over 1,600 tons of food had been preserved by WIs across Britain, reaching an impressive total of 5,300 tons in 1945.

Women's Institutes also helped to billet evacuees in rural areas, collected herbs and other plants for medicinal purposes, and wild rosehips to be made into syrup: a crucial source of Vitamin C for children as the supply of imported oranges was cut off. They also ran market stalls to sell surplus fruit and vegetables. There are no references to these activities in the New Barkby records, but a 'War Knitting' party was established in October 1939 at Shepherd's Hey on The Meadway, the home of the New Barkby branch President, Mrs F.M. Angrave. Proceeds from refreshments were used to buy wool to make gloves and socks for servicemen, and over 50 members volunteered to help with the knitting – contributing to a national total of over 150,000 garments and other 'comforts' for the troops produced by WI members. A request in October 1940 for the WI to show a film by the National Allotment Society, *A Garden Goes to War*, was declined on the grounds that its members were not allotment holders; but from January 1941 the Hall was loaned free of charge for 'work of national importance', and later used to show Ministry of Information films.

There are also occasional references to the WI's role in disseminating information and advice on making the most of limited wartime resources. In November 1943, for instance, the branch was asked by the Ministry of Labour to help with a 'Scrap-Metal Drive 'for the making of war armaments', by informing its local representative of sources of

scrap metal and reminding 'all those who may be interested that the locators will call on them in the near future'. WI 'demonstrators' gave lectures or classes on a wide range of subjects during the war to help maximise the available resources. Topics included keeping rabbits for food and fur, haybox cookery, and crafts to make new clothes from old. Edna Smith recalled a demonstration on making slippers out of old felt hats, with soles crocheted in string. In July 1943, owing to the difficulty of getting a demonstrator for the September meeting, members of the Committee itself were asked to give some 'Helpful Hints' on wartime cookery 'or any other useful subject'. The NFWI also organised courses on a national basis, including a series of 12 lectures on 'The Domestic Front' early in 1943. These were intended to 'train members in all branches of household thrift', enabling them to pass on the information in turn to 'all housewives in the district'. By May 1941, however - when the catering for its regular Whist Drives was 'becoming very difficult' - the branch had to make economies of its own. It was agreed to limit the refreshments to either sandwiches or cakes, with six Committee members 'in alphabetical order' supplying cake for alternate Whist Drives.

The summer outing planned for 1940 – a trip into the local countryside - was abandoned due to 'the present uncertain state of the country', and in 1942 the branch took issue with the National Federation over the WI Annual Meeting at the Albert Hall in London. Declaring this to be 'unnecessary' owing to 'restrictions in travelling and other war-time conditions', it declined to send a delegate and made the same decision on the same grounds in the following year. Closer to home, in December 1944 its drama group, the New Barkby WI Players, presented three one act plays produced by Mrs Angrave, Mrs Harper, Miss Gordon and Miss Hughes – *Women at War*, *O.H.M.S.*, and *The Shadow Passes*' - to 'a large audience' in the church hall in aid of the Red Cross. By no means the whole of WI meetings were taken up with war-related matters, however. In line with the NFWI policy of 'providing for the members a centre of tranquillity and cheerfulness in a sadly troubled world', there is an air of normality about many of their activities. In

November 1944, for instance, the *Leicester Evening Mail* reported that a lecture was given on 'The Effect of Colour' by Miss Garner of Leicester. The 'social half hour' was provided by Mrs. J. Sanderson and Mrs Sykes, and the competition was won by Mrs. A. Baldwin and Mrs. R. Brookhouse.

DIG FOR VICTORY

Individuals were also encouraged to play their part in securing food supplies. The 'Dig for Victory' campaign was introduced by the Ministry of Agriculture in October 1939 to encourage people to grow their own food, using gardens, public parks and other open spaces for the purpose – with the help of numerous leaflets advising those with little or no previous experience. By the end of the war there were approximately one and a half million allotment holders in Britain producing 10% of its food. There were several allotment sites in Syston during World War Two. The largest, the only one that now remains, was situated towards the end of Upper Church Street and divided into 74 large allotments. There were also allotments off Goodes Lane and some (on land owned by the railway) off Broad Street. The allotments on Barkby Road behind the cemetery were privately owned, and a small field at the back of the Styles was also given over by a local farmer for use as allotments for the duration of the war. George Toon's family lived on Barkby Road, and his father had an allotment on this site where George used to help him grow vegetables. George was the oldest of four children, and although he was 17 when war was declared he was never called up as he was severely deaf.

Allotments on the main site were rented from the Parish Council, with strict regulations about their use. In April 1941 one tenant was found to be sub-letting the land to her son-in-law, and someone else was cultivating another part of it. The Parish Council decided 'it would not be fair to turn him off now he has got the ground in good condition and has set it', but new tenants were henceforth required to sign an agreement not to sub-let. Roundhill Modern School produced food on its own plots of land. It was reported in April 1941 that in the previous season this amounted to three and a half tons of potatoes, 500 lbs of cabbage, 70 lb

of turnips, 37 lb of parsnips, and six hundredweight of swedes. Harrison's seed merchants also ran seed growing trials at Syston during the war, growing different species side by side to compare them. According to a newspaper report in July 1944, these included onions from North and South America, around 20 varieties of cabbages and broad beans, English and foreign peas, and different varieties of lettuce 'which have been greatly improved'.

A large garden was a great advantage. With the help of relatives and friends, as Jane Marshall recalled, the Talbott family garden:

> 'was put to good use growing vegetables and all kinds of different fruits. We ate what was in season and the fruits were preserved by bottling or made into jam. Potatoes were stored under the bed in the dark and apples were stored in trays in the shed. It all seemed normal at the time! Baskets of eggs were bought from Key's Farm in Barkby and preserved in water glass [sodium silicate]'.

Vivienne Everitt (nee Garner) recalled the family garden in The Nook as:

> 'huge, with every fruit tree and bush you could imagine, including a famous Syston White plum tree: I can still taste it now! During the summer Mum would sell fruit over the garden gate. The garden was so big that after the war the Council compulsorily purchased some of it to build flats on'.

Late in the war, their own rations were supplemented by parcels of lemons, limes and coconuts, sent by Vivienne's father who was serving at a Royal Air Force staging post in Sierra Leone.

FUNDS FOR THE WAR EFFORT

A great deal of fundraising went on in Syston during the war, both as part of wider national or local campaigns, and to provide 'comforts' for men and women serving in the forces, such as warm knitted gloves, balaclava helmets and scarves. One of the earliest was the Syston Spitfire Fund, established in September 1940. This got off to a good start with a donation of £55 from Mr Eatough, owner of Eatough's footwear factory, and had raised £487 10s 4d by the time it closed in December that year.* All the money was passed on to the Leicester and County Spitfire Fund, administered by the Lord Mayor of Leicester, which donated seven Spitfires to the national effort.

During War Weapons Week in June 1941, £24,000 of Syston's target of £30,000 was raised within a few days, thanks to a variety of attractions as well as contributions from local organisations and employers. An RAF plane was on display at the Recreation Ground, and visitors were 'privileged to inspect the cockpit of the machine' for the price of a 6d savings stamp, raising £3 9s in the process. According to the *Leicester Advertiser* on 7 June 1941, a competition to guess the weight of a night bomber's wheel proved 'very attractive', and the winning guess by Mr Tom Scoton was only two and a half pounds short of the actual weight of a hundred and forty four and a half pounds. The tickets for a raffle to win groceries were drawn from a cooling drum salvaged from a Spitfire. Other events included an exhibition of children's posters at the Infant and Junior Schools, and a dance at the Assembly Rooms on the Friday evening that raised over £20, with music by Ted Smith's Rhythm Swingers. Employees of Eatough's contributed over £1,000, easily exceeding their own target of £225 (representing £5 an hour for a 45 hour week).

The week ended with a 'grand parade' from Thurmaston to Syston along Leicester Road and High Street to The Green, which included soldiers and a band, two Bren gun carriers, Home Guard and ARP personnel, fire-fighting apparatus, and motor tractors driven by Land Girls. The salute was taken by Brigadier J. S. Osmond MBE MC from a platform decorated with flags. 'Keen rivalry' between Syston and nearby villages, along with a 'glorious rush of saving' towards the end of the week, brought the total raised to £59,996. This was originally announced as £65,000, before it was found that one large sum had been counted twice – but the lower figure still represented a contribution of £12 per head of the population, a remarkable achievement. Syston also raised funds for other national initiatives, including Warship Week in

1942, Wings for Victory Week in the following year, and Salute the Soldier Week in 1944, beating its target of £30,000 for the latter by over £13,000.

Children made their own efforts to raise money for the war effort. In December 1941 Brian Allen of St Peter's Street and an evacuee friend from Bristol raised £2 by holding a 'library', donating half to the Syston Red Cross Agriculture Fund and half to the same fund for Bristol. In June of that year, seven year old Philip Barter, who was disabled and had missed out on the distribution of Red Cross collecting boxes to local children, found his own novel way of raising funds. Picking up an empty box from the floor of his parents' grocery shop in Leicester Road, the *Leicester Advertiser* reported, he 'crayoned a big red cross on the lid, and cut a slit big enough to take pennies. Grandma was the first "victim", then mother and father, and when the customers on the shop heard about it the pennies simply "rolled in"…'. The Red Cross Committee later wrote him a letter of thanks, appointed him an Honorary Voluntary Associate of the British Red Cross – and sent him a real collecting box that attracted 'a regular stream of callers to put money in'. In May 1941 Harry Payne (9), the son of the Parish Clerk, offered a prize of seven books to raise £1 for the Waifs and Strays Society, to help children bombed out of their homes; and in September 1943, Roy Taylor of Fosseway and Alvin Muggleton of Wanlip Road, both 13, raised 7s 3d for the Aid to Russia Fund by holding a film show.

Funds were also raised throughout the war to provide 'comforts' or other gifts for local servicemen and women. In the autumn of 1939 the New Barkby Women's Conservative Association held a series of Whist Drives, using the proceeds to send 'Christmas cheer to Syston and New Barkby men in the Forces'. Proceeds from refreshments were also used to buy wool to make gloves and socks for servicemen, over 50 members volunteering to help with the knitting. Other local organisations held competitions to raise money for the Syston Comforts Fund, which was established in January 1940. This was chaired by Mr E. Quinn, and had 40 committee members representing a variety of organisations and employers in the village. Over

400 people attended a concert organised by the Comforts Fund in August 1940, just one of many events for which it was directly responsible. One of the more unusual was a competition in April 1945 that raised £30 with a prize of 2lbs of tea, sent home by Leading Aircraftman Walter Lewin who was serving with the RAF in Ceylon. Many other organisations also contributed to the fund - including the Syston and District Fanciers Club, which was offering competition prizes of onions, apples and a live rabbit in January 1944. So many village organisations ran their own Comfort Funds that the Parish Council called for a more systematic approach in April 1944 with a 'pooling' of the money that they raised. The 'whole idea was wrong', one of its members said: 'The public houses, clubs and churches each had separate funds, with the result that some of the Forces got plenty and others only a little'.

At the same meeting it was reported that over 500 postal orders of 10s each had so far been sent to servicemen and women, and 'stacks of letters' of thanks received from them in turn. A new fund – the Syston Services Fund, chaired by Charles Lewin - was set up in January 1945 to raise £2,000 'or more' through events and house-to-house collections, to give each Syston serviceman and woman £5 when they returned home. However, not all the funds raised in Syston during the war went to the war effort itself. Local Scouts continued to raise money for their building fund, and the annual subscription of £10 for the 'Syston Cot' at the Queen Alexandra Hospital in Mandalay, Burma was raised as usual in 1940, despite Miss Holmes being unable to 'present the usual play during Lent' due to wartime conditions. 'Where there's a will there's a way, the parish magazine reported in October that year: 'Miss Holmes proved this by informing her usual subscribers and a few other friends of the dilemma and they have rallied round'. Regular fundraising for the Leicester Royal Infirmary also continued, one notable effort being the £1 13s 3d raised in October 1944 'for a giant pear' weighing one and a half pounds – whether by an auction or a 'guess the weight' competition, the newspaper report does not say.

A note on wartime sums of money - for ease of reading, and because the results vary according to what is being compared (prices of goods and services, purchasing power, or average earnings, for example), no attempt has been made to convert wartime sums of money into current equivalents. Websites such as https://www.measuringworth. com/ppoweruk/ can be used for this purpose if desired.

Syston Comforts Fund
1945

Although we have now got Peace the people of Syston are still mindful of those who have not yet been fortunate enough to return to their homes. As a token of appreciation for all you have done the Comforts Fund ask you to accept the enclosed P.O. (10/-), with Greetings and Best Wishes for a safe and early return.

For and on behalf of the Committee.

E. QUINN
Chairman

J. E. BUCKLEY
Vice-Chairman

J. W. ARNOLD
Hon. Treasurer

B. J. BOWERS
Hon. Secretary
54 Broad Street, Syston

5 CHALLENGING TIMES – VILLAGE LIFE IN WARTIME

CHURCHES AND CHAPELS

Places of worship played a central role in village life before the war, both for their own congregations and others who used them as meeting places. This became still more important once the war started, as those left behind suffered losses or long periods of separation and uncertainty. Prayers were regularly said for villagers serving in the military or ancillary forces for their safety or recovery from wounds, and news of them was passed on at services or through the *Parish Magazine* and similar publications. Rev Tetley, the vicar of Syston from 1940, is also described in a directory in 1941 as 'honorary chaplain to the Forces'.

Special services of remembrance and intercession were held as the war continued. In August 1941 Rev Tetley introduced a 'Rose Service' at St Peter's at which he read out a Roll of Honour with the names of people from the village serving in the forces. This attracted a 'crowded congregation', including a large number of the parents and wives of servicemen and women. Each person attending the service was invited to bring a 'rose of remembrance', and these were placed at the foot of the altar during the singing of a hymn. The Syston Feast in mid-July was a regular event in the church calendar, the occasion for a fundraising fete as well as a special service in the church, and on this occasion in 1941 Rev Tetley also revived the 'ancient custom' of a 'Procession of Witness' to the church for the service at which he preached. At Syston Methodist Church in High Street, Rev Clarence O. Ward also held services of intercession on Wednesday evenings where the names of servicemen were read out. These are described in the church history as 'well attended, intimate, moving and a comfort to all concerned'. The services were continued by Rev Ward's successor, Rev Bernard Sheldon, who also instituted a comforts fund: 'his letters and postal orders went to all theatres of war'.

In the early stages of the war Rev Tetley's predecessor Rev T.R.J. (Thomas) Avery had been asked to organise a comforts fund to send parcels to local men and women serving in the armed forces. He was cautious about taking this on, having set up a fund for the same purpose in the First World War that 'then became more than one could manage'. Writing in the *Parish Magazine* in December 1939, he suggested that each group in the village:

> 'should get together, and combine, otherwise I fear some will have more than one parcel, whilst others have none. I only throw this out as a suggestion. This to my mind *should be a village effort*. Further, I suggest that a Treasurer be appointed, to whom we poor men who cannot knit, might give a donation'.

His advice was taken and the Syston Comforts Fund was formed in January 1940 to co-ordinate the efforts of local organisations. Later that year, Rev Avery left Syston for a new appointment as Rector of Lutterworth. In the parish magazine he described his time in the village as 'one long happy memory… He expressed most cordially his thanks and appreciation to all parishioners for the very devoted and loyal support he had received'. Mrs Avery was also thanked for her own contribution to the village, including her involvement in the Infant Welfare organisation 'from its inception… [she] had nursed hundreds of babies and loved doing so!'.

Surviving copies of the parish magazine from 1939 - 1941 give a sense of other church activities during this period, and the people associated with them. In August 1940, for instance, it reported that Robert MacLaren Todd, assistant organist at the church for eight years, had passed his final medical examinations after graduating in Natural Sciences from Trinity College, Cambridge and completing his training at St Bart's hospital in London. The son of local chemist Robert A. MacLaren Todd of Melton Road, in July 1941 he was appointed as resident Medical Officer at the City General Hospital in Leicester. In September 1940 the

Price 2d.   MAY, 1940.

SS. PETER AND PAUL
(SYSTON)
Parish Magazine.

Clergy:
Vicar's Warden: Mr. H. S. TEMPEST.   Parish Warden: Mr. R. McLAREN TODD.
Parish Clerk: Mr. ERNEST PAYNE, The Green.

Parish Church Sunday Services.

Holy Communion, 8 a.m. (1st Sunday *also* after Morning Prayer.)
Morning Prayer, 10-45.   Evensong 6-30.
Children's Service, 1st Sunday 9-15.   Infants, 3rd Sunday, 2-15.

S. Aidan's Services.

Holy Communion, 3rd Sunday, 9 a.m.   Evensong every Sunday, 6-30.
Sunday School—Morning, 10   Afternoon, Juniors 2 ; Seniors, 3.

Syston Parish Magazine May 1940 – life carries on.

Magazine also carried news of a former member of the congregation, Jack Fernsby, who had recently been ordained as a deacon by the Lord Bishop of Durham and appointed to the village church of Billingham-on-Tees in County Durham. He was the son of Frederick and Emma Fernsby and twin brother of Guy, who served in the Royal Air Force Volunteer Reserve and died in an accident in 1944.

The church hall was also widely used for meetings and theatrical performances, among them a pantomime in December 1941 entitled *The Joyous Adventures of Abou Hassan*, presented by the Syston Players. This was described by the *Syston and District Times* as 'a delightful musical comedy' with 'many pretty scenes', including the singing of *I'm Forever Blowing Bubbles* and *Happy Days are Here Again* in the Caliph's palace as part of the finale. The pantomime was produced by Mr W.H. Frost, a teacher at the village Junior School who had a close connection with Syston's other Anglican church, St Aidan's. This was opened in 1900 on Wanlip Road as a 'mission church' and was still referred to as such in the parish magazine in September 1939. Its congregations at this time had increased, the magazine reported, and it was 'filling a need in the Wanlip Road and neighbourhood'. In April 1940 John Sharp, who had conducted services at St Aidan's 'for some time… freely and willingly', left to join the Grenadier Guards: 'He loved his work. We know that wherever he goes he will be an influence for that which is good'. Mr Frost, 'who possesses the Archbishop's Certificate [the Archbishop of Canterbury's Certificate in Church Music] will help out'. In *Syston as I Remember It*, Frank Astill recalled another of Mr Frost's productions in April that year: a play entitled *The Legend of Tea* in which he and 'many others, Harry Payne and his brother Bernard included' took part. Frank also sang in the church choir, 'and on many occasions after choir practice we were seconded to the choir mistress's house to work on her croquet course, which was near New Zealand Lane'.

Rev Tetley was also much occupied during the war in conducting weddings, sometimes two or three in the same day, many of them between local women and men serving in the armed forces. Presumably at least some of these were fitted into short periods of leave, or in advance of a posting overseas – and other such marriages took place in smaller numbers at the Methodist church on High Street, the Primitive Methodist chapel on Melton Road, and the Baptist chapel on Leicester Road. Late in 1943 the ladies of the Methodist and Baptist churches also organised a Services Canteen at the Primitive Methodist schoolrooms. This was open every weekday evening until around 10 pm and supplied tea, coffee, biscuits and sandwiches. This service was said to be much appreciated by the troops stationed in the area, particularly the Americans. In December 1944 the *Leicester Evening Mail* reported that its first anniversary was celebrated by inviting 70 soldiers and Auxiliary Territorial Service (ATS) women who used the canteen to a supper and entertainment by a Thurmaston concert party.

High Street Methodist Church – a 1950s view with Walker's timber storage adjoining. *(Ken Asher)*

Some of the men and women from High Street Methodist Church serving in HM Forces in October 1944 can be identified from a list of names pasted into a *Shorter Book of Offices*. Among them were Sylvia Dixon, Alan Ferens Batty, a local doctor who had joined the Royal Air Force in 1941, and three brothers from each of the Lewin and Reid families.

SYSTON RED CROSS

The British Red Cross joined forces with St John's Ambulance Brigade at the start of the war to form the Joint War Organisation. It played a crucial role

Taylorcraft workers, March 1944 – a ladies' football match which raised £14 for Red Cross funds.
(Leicester Mercury Group)

in providing services for the sick and wounded at home, and civilians needing help due to enemy action, as well as for Prisoners of War abroad. It also trained civilians including ARP units in First Aid, providing classes, manuals and First Aid kits.

The Syston Red Cross branch held its meetings in the old Baptist Church on Chapel Street. Mrs Winefried Payne, who lived on The Green, was the local Cadet Officer at that time and for a number of years after the end of the war. Margaret Thompson, who lived on Central Avenue, joined the Red Cross at the age of ten in 1944 and recalls Mrs Payne as 'a very senior officer. Doreen West was another officer and Doreen Smith a senior cadet. I remember that when I was eleven a cadet died and we formed a guard of honour at her funeral'. Pre-war a uniform was needed to become a cadet, but this requirement was suspended from 1941, and any clean, tidy clothing such as school uniform was acceptable.

The Red Cross was wholly dependent on volunteers and public fund-raising, and many local organisations and individuals did their bit to support it throughout the war. Its Penny-a-Week scheme made a major contribution to the provision of food parcels for Allied Prisoners of War and soldiers serving abroad, and often benefitted from collections and fundraising events in Syston. Mary Poyner (nee Payne) remembers 'going from house to house collecting for the Red Cross. We asked people for 1d a week, and I used to collect up the Avenues. I remember getting very cold in the winter doing this'. In August 1941 the *Syston and District Times* reported that:

'Syston children are making full use of their school holidays by organising efforts towards the Penny-a-Week funds. On Saturday a concert was given in an outbuilding at the rear of houses in Upper Church Street, when the programme included the pantomime "Cinderella", songs, duets and two sketches, "The Washerwoman's Mistake", and "A Love Affair". The producer was Jack Reid, the stage manager Teddy Toon'.

During the interval tea and cakes 'made by neighbours and parents' were served, and the sum of 13s 9d was raised. The performance was repeated 'with success' on the following Monday. A garden fete held in Chapel Street by 'two little girls', E. Bolton and M. Woods, also raised over £2 for the fund, while Barbara Lewin, aged 13, 'held a hoop-la stall for three nights and collected 17s'. Invitations to village events were extended to members of the Forces at the Red Cross convalescent home at Brooksby Hall, among them one from New Barkby Women's Institute to attend its Thursday afternoon Whist Drive in February 1942.

The Red Cross *Year Book* for 1941 noted that the Leicestershire Association had also 'staffed station rest rooms which has proved a boon to Forces passing through'. In towns and cities that were bombed, Red Cross and St John's members worked alongside Civil Defence first aid squads to help the wounded. Among them was the Syston-born woman Rosa Lord, a St John's nursing sister before the war, who was awarded the British Empire Medal in the summer of 1941 for her work in charge of the First Aid post at St Philip's church on Evington Road, Leicester. According to the Medical Officer of Health, Dr E.K. McDonald, for the whole of the war so far she had 'organised the post in what can only be described as an extraordinarily efficient manner'.

MEMORIES OF SCOUTING IN SYSTON DURING WORLD WAR II

Dot Wilkes was an Assistant Cub Master with Syston Scouts until she joined the WAAF in 1942. These are her memories of the local Scout troop in wartime.

'Syston has had a Scout group since 1908. It met at various venues until they had their own hall built in Oxford Street in 1938. Following the outbreak of World War II, most of the older scouts, together with Mr Moore (Group Scoutmaster), Frank Mc Pherson (Assistant Scoutmaster), and Herbert Byatt (Cubmaster) became members of the First Aid Squad at Syston Air Raid Precautions' Station, which is where I first met these men. Herbert Byatt was assisted by cousins Joan and Nancy Cook, but in 1940 Joan planned to get married, which would leave the Cubs short of one Assistant Leader. Mr Moore decided that I would make a suitable replacement for Joan, and after some persuasion on his part I agreed to give it a try. I didn't really know what I was letting myself in for as I'd never even been a Girl Guide, and in fact Syston did not have a Guide troop in those days!

'Before being invested as a Scout I had to pass the "Tenderfoot Test". This consisted of learning the Law and the Promise, how to tie six different knots, the uses of the Scout Staff and how to build a bivouac. This all had to be done to Mr Moore's (Skip's) satisfaction. All the Wolf Cubs had to pass this same test before going on to work for various badges. Basic scouting skills such as pioneering, backwoods cooking, First Aid, knots and lashings were a large part of the training programme along with knowledge about personal hygiene, diet and exercise. The Cubs met in the newly built Syston Scout Headquarters in Oxford Street (an unadopted road in those days). The big meeting room was heated by a large cast iron stove which was fuelled by coke and was very difficult to light, giving out lots of smoke and not much heat.

'Syston Scouts' Band kept going throughout the war in one way or another depending on who was available to play and lead. Scouts went out round Syston with the 'trek cart' (a large and rather heavy hand cart) collecting salvage for the war effort and collected barrow-loads of newspapers for recycling. The yearly camping trips also kept going, although the wartime restrictions put a stop to camping at the coast between 1940 and 1944 when it was considered unsafe to go there. Petrol rationing was also in force so camps from 1940 to 45 were held at Saxby, which is about five miles east of Melton Mowbray. The Scouts loaded up the trek cart with all the equipment and walked to Saxby, which took about a day. Working with the Syston Scouts, I got used to older Scouts and Rover Scouts being with us for one event and suddenly gone by the next as they had been called up. Inevitably news came

Syston British Legion – the opening of the new headquarters in 1949 by Lord Cromwell.
(Leicester Mercury Group)

from time to time of the loss or imprisonment of someone we knew; but this was a fact of life in wartime and had to be accepted.*

'I remained as Assistant Cubmaster (the title of Cubmistress did not exist in those days) until I was old enough to join the WAAF in 1942, and Herbert Byatt and Nancy Cook carried on after I left. I attended meetings whenever I was home on leave, and kept my hand in by going along to pack meetings if possible wherever I happened to be stationed. In February 1943 I was presented with my first Warrant as Assistant Cubmaster, and after I returned to Syston when I left the WAAF, I rejoined Syston Scout Group'.

Dorothea Wilkes, Honorary Commissioner, July 2015

* Former Scouts from Syston who died during the

war were Victor Clarke, William Iliffe, William Ernest Lewin and Alan Walker.

As a footnote, much of the money for the new Scout Hall was raised by a Ladies Committee chaired by Mrs McLaren Todd. She and her husband, the local chemist, were both 'keenly interested' in the Scouts, as the *Leicester Advertiser* reported in November 1939, and marked their Silver Wedding anniversary by presenting a set of crockery for use at social events in the Scouts' HQ.

SYSTON BRITISH LEGION

The local branch of the British Legion found a clear role during the war in fulfilling the objectives of the national organisation. This was founded in 1921 to promote 'the welfare and interests of current and former members of British armed forces' and 'to care for those who had suffered as a result of service in armed forces during the war, whether through their own service or through that of a husband, father or son'. The Syston branch was inaugurated in 1932, and had a membership at that time of around 200. Many of its wartime activities focused on the families of members, including a film show in December 1939 at the local cinema, the Savoy. Over 120 children were present, including boys from the Manor House children's home in New Barkby. Instead of the usual festive tea party each child received 'a parcel of Christmas cheer.' In November 1941 the British Legion was responsible for establishing a Garden of Remembrance on the recreation ground. Along with the Syston Comfort Fund, the branch was also involved in running the 'Holidays at Home' scheme in Syston in 1943, one of many such schemes intended to offer a break from normal routine as petrol rationing and the risk of bombing made holidays elsewhere more and more difficult.

At the outbreak of war the branch still had no premises of its own. Meetings were held in the Church Hall or public houses in the village, and many of its wartime efforts were directed to building up funds for a Legion Headquarters in Syston, in anticipation of the greater demand it would face from ex-servicemen and women and their families once the war was over. As its Chairman, Mr W.J. Prince put it, there was a need for:

> 'a home of our own where ex-servicemen can meet to play games together, as they have fought together, and where the spirit of comradeship can be fostered. We shall carry on and do our job until our serving men return, and we will then hand over to them to carry on the good work of the Legion, but we shall always support them in any plans they make'.

A Building Committee was established early in the war and bought land for this purpose adjoining

Syston British Red Cross – on parade in High Street. *(Marc Williams)*

39

the Savoy Cinema. At the branch annual meeting in October 1944 it was noted that £281 3s 3d had been raised so far towards the building itself. By November 1946 membership had increased to 370, including many ex-servicemen; and 'success in pensions appeals' was also reported. However, it was not until 1948 that a pre-fabricated concrete building was erected on the site. The 'hut,' as it was known locally, was officially opened in the following year by Lord Cromwell. It was heated by a cast iron pot-bellied stove in the centre, and those lucky enough to position themselves near to the stove were warm (or even hot), whilst those on the edges of the hut remained cold. As membership continued to increase over the years, the 'hut' became inadequate, and it was replaced with a modern brick building on the same site in the 1960s.

CLUBS AND THE ADULT SCHOOL

The effects of the war on other organisations in Syston were variable. Recreational clubs such as the Wreake Angling Club and the Syston and District Fanciers' Society continued during the war without a great deal or disruption, despite the call up of members or Civil Defence Duties. The latter held its usual competitive shows of pigeons and poultry at the Queen Victoria Hotel, and winners in the different categories were regularly reported in the local press. The Men's Bowling Club also continued as usual, but the war took its toll on the bowling green itself. In June 1944 the Club complained to the Parish Council about its condition, but the Council 'did not think they should spend more in wages' on it: income from the green did not cover the costs and was subsidised from the rates. The Bowling Club pointed out that there would be no income at all if they could not use it, to which the Chairman of the Parish Council replied: 'Then it would go derelict, and there would be no expense at all'. A compromise was eventually agreed, with the Club offering to assist with maintaining the green.

One organisation that did experience significant difficulties during the war was the Syston Men's Adult School on Melton Road, of which Mr J.E. Buckley was both Chairman and President. This had previously played a lively part in village life, but appears to have been in something of a decline by the 1930s. Reference was made in March 1939 to three 'small funds' that had been wound up: namely the Library, Choir, and Family Party Funds, while the Minutes of the May 1942 meeting refer to 'decreased activities'. The 'Old Folks Tea' had not been held since 1940, and 'other social occasions were practically nil'. However, the hall itself was still being used regularly. It was let for a dance party every Saturday night throughout the year, and its snooker tables were also very popular. As a teenager, Frank Astill remembered Saturday evenings as the 'stute night':

> 'The Caretaker was George… Inside were about six to eight full size snooker tables. We were allowed to play on the first two, the rest were for the older men. George was good for two fags for 3d, and while we were waiting for a table to be vacant we would play Pontoon or Brag… After getting fish and chips at Dyers next door to Peberday's, we'd go home'.

The Minutes of the November 1943 meeting of the Adult School refer once again to reduced activities for several years past, which had been 'precipitated still further by the war.' At this meeting it was decided to sell its 'effects' (i.e. the furnishings), and in April 1946 the sale of the premises themselves was being considered. However, it was agreed that 'although the School was only just holding together at present it would be a pity to sell out and a distinct breach of faith with those gentlemen who had done so much for the School in the past… a special attempt was to be made to revive the School… [it was] suggested that the buildings should not be sold, at least until such time as the outcome of the attempt at revival was seen'.

Syston British Red Cross – Leicestershire Youth Detachment 500 October 1943. *(Marc Williams)*

6 EKEING OUT AND MAKING DO – RATIONING AND SHORTAGES

PETROL RATIONING

Rationing began early in the Second World War to protect supplies of imported goods at risk from enemy action and those essential to the war effort. Petrol rationing was introduced in September 1939 and continued until 1950. Coupons were valid only for the month of issue to prevent hoarding, and in the summer of 1942 the small allowance for private motorists was withdrawn altogether.

This was just one of the challenges faced by Mary Timson and Ernest Gamble when they were married at Thurmaston parish church in September 1942. The photographer from Leicester 'would not be able to come to the church', she recalled: 'because he had not got enough petrol to get him to Thurmaston and he had used up his monthly ration'. Their reception was held at St Martin's School in Friar Lane in Leicester, so 'the best he could do was to get permission for us to stand in the playground of Alderman Newton School, with the Cathedral as a background. Fortunately this was only a short distance from Friar Lane'. Betty Goodwill and Bert Simpson experienced a different 'solution' to the fuel shortage when they went on their honeymoon in August 1941. The 'home-made taxi' that transported them from Buxton station to the farmhouse where they were staying for their honeymoon 'ran on the owner's "own mixture" as there was no available petrol. Our hosts heard us coming from miles away…'.

While streets almost empty of cars became new playgrounds for children, local bus services were also restricted to save fuel, and adults relying on them for travel experienced many frustrations. The main service between Syston and Leicester was operated by the Midland Red bus company, but a prepayment system for tickets introduced in January 1942 'aroused considerable criticism'. There must be 'hundreds of the [previous] red tickets still in the hands of the villagers which were a dead loss to them since the date for expiry had now passed', the

Parish Council Chairman, Ernest Quinn, said of this. Office workers travelling later in the morning now had to pay the equivalent of 70% extra, while those going home for lunch had to pay out two shillings a day for the journey. Another member of the Parish Council, Mr Newton, described the changes as 'sheer dictatorship, and he was prepared to kick against that sort of thing every time', but the bus company itself had little choice in these matters. Its activities were regulated by the Traffic Commissioners, and they were dismissive of the letter of 'protest' that the Parish Council sent to them.

These arrangements were intended to discourage 'non-essential' travel – or in the words of the Midland Red itself later that year, to ensure that 'the regular five or six day worker should not be crowded out by casual passengers, whether pleasure seekers, shoppers, or workers using the services on wet days only'. However, complaints about 'inadequate' bus services from Leicester surfaced again in February 1944. As the threat of bombing receded, people began to venture further afield in the evenings, but it took some time for services to catch up with the greater demand. On one particular evening the last bus (which left Leicester at 9.10 pm) was full by the time it reached Melton Turn, leaving around 35 Syston passengers stranded there and at Checketts Road. This was attributed to people taking their children to the pantomime in Leicester and 'packing the bus' on the way back!

FOOD RATIONING

The need to conserve food supplies and increase production of food at home led to the rationing of bacon, ham, sugar and butter in January 1940, followed by meat in March that year, and tea in July. Many other items were rationed as the war continued, including cheese, eggs, rice, jam, treacle, dried fruit and sweets. In the circumstances, waste was to be avoided at all costs, hence the *Leicester Advertiser* felt it worth reporting in June 1940 that one Syston housewife had 'got her own back' on the ants that had attacked her treacle ration: 'having climbed five feet up the wall to the food cupboard... Pouring the contaminated part of the syrup into an empty tin and adding a little hot water, she placed it outside the doorway and in a few hours had trapped hundreds of the pests'.

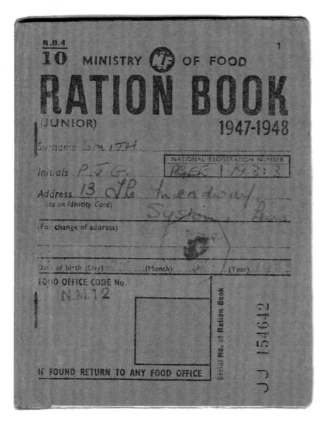

Junior Ration Book issued to local boy
Perry Smith, 1947.

Once rationing started people had to register with their chosen shops – several different ones selling different commodities - and shopkeepers were provided with enough food to supply them. While the amount of rations was strictly controlled, the choice of shopkeeper could make life easier in other ways. Eileen Freer , who lived in Lower Church Street, recalled that: 'Mum had some property in Jamaica, and whilst she was waiting for Dad's money and the rent of the property she used to send us to Sheffield's [butcher] to collect the meat, and he used to put it on tick until her money came'.

Monica Naylor's parents kept a grocery and greengrocery shop on Leicester Road during the war. 'Large families registered half with shops like ours', she recalls: 'where they could often exchange

their butter ration for margarine. The other half were registered at the Co-op on High Street. I believe I grew to be good with figures as the whole family used to sort and count ration coupons at the end of each month'. They lived next door to a butcher's shop, but 'got no privileges'. The best meat 'was taken by Ratcliffe College', and the family had to queue like everyone else for goods like oranges or bananas that arrived 'intermittently' and were not available in their own shop. Jane Marshall's mother told her that she was once:

'left in my pram outside Mrs Raleigh's greengrocery shop and she had let us have some bananas, which were virtually impossible to obtain during the war. I decided that maybe the passers by might like to see them so waved them around. My Mother was not best pleased. I also remember us receiving a box of tinned foods containing such things as the famous Spam, tinned fruits etc – I think they were sent over from the USA'.

Marjorie Clowes (nee North), whose parents ran the Blue Bell pub on Melton Road in the later years of the war, remembers:

'6.30 am queues at the Co-op butchers and greengrocers' in High Street. Liver and potted beef were sometimes available; small amounts of butter and lard... no oranges or bananas. I don't think that we were particularly affected, but I missed fresh fruit. However, once the American forces arrived at Gaddesby, they used to come into Syston for a night out, (particularly on Saturday nights) and come to the pub. They would bring gifts of tinned fruit and sugar etc to the pub for my parents. The Baker's Arms pub (on the corner of Barkby Road and Leicester Road), would not allow black American soldiers in, but they were always welcomed at the Bell. We'd registered for groceries at Wells' shop which was on the same side of the road as the pub, but a little bit nearer to High Street. They sold bacon and groceries'.

Regulations around rationing were complex, and some local shopkeepers fell foul of the law, usually through pressure of work or misunderstanding rather than a deliberate intent to break them. One local butcher was summoned in January 1942 for supplying meat to customers without coupons – something that he said was 'an oversight'. He was understaffed and his wife, who was responsible for keeping the books, 'had her housework to do. This was the only error in food registering at his business'. The magistrates accepted the explanation and took a 'lenient view', fining him £1 and 10 shillings costs. In January 1945 another Syston butcher appeared in court on five counts of 'preparing sale tickets regarding the proposed sale of meat at an excessive price', and one of 'delivering meat without a statement of nett weight'. In his defence he said he had over 380 registered customers, and his son was away in the forces: 'It must be through not looking properly. I have to do it all alone'. The magistrates could have imposed fines of up to £100, but his 'good record' over 40 years in the trade was taken into account, and he was only fined £2 for each of the ticket offences and £1 for the delivery. In July 1945 a local farmer was also prosecuted for 'obtaining more milk than authorised, and failing to notify an excess quantity'. He admitted selling up to 30 gallons more than permitted in each of two weeks, rather than informing the Regional Food Officer so the additional supply could be redirected, and was fined £10 with £3 3s costs.

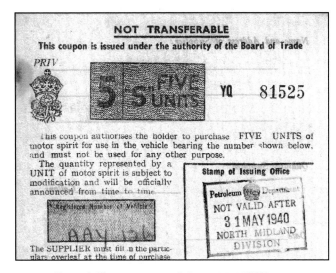

Petrol Coupon issued for a 16-19HP car.

The day to day challenges posed by rationing were greatly increased in the case of wartime weddings, where guests still had to be provided with an appropriate level of hospitality. Having set the date,

arranged for the banns to be read, and secured the venue, Mary Gamble recalled of her wedding to Ernest in September 1942: 'Now our problems really began'. They decided to do the catering themselves, with the aid of some 'very expensive champagne' supplied by her father's cousin, a businessman in Leicester, and his wife, who worked for a wholesale grocer. Each week:

> 'she would bring us various items of food, such as butter, sugar, tea or cheese, sometimes a tin of salmon or fruit – all supposed to be on ration. This was illegal, so I was a bit worried that we would end up in prison instead of at the altar. All the family also tried to save a little of their rations each week, so that we could make some sandwiches. Dad also grew tomatoes and cucumbers in the greenhouse, and lettuce and onions in the garden, so we were able to make a decent salad. Eggs were in very short supply, but another friend kept hens and let us have a few so that we could bake some cakes and biscuits. The wedding cake was a Victoria sponge, made by a professional baker who lived not far from us, in Humberstone Lane in Thurmaston. He covered the cake with a circular box made of cardboard and decorated with icing so it looked like a real wedding cake'.

Bread was not rationed until after the war, but as David Borderick remembers, the 'National Loaf' introduced in the autumn of 1942 was 'a terrible colour because they were allowed to put bran in that normally had been fed to livestock. It was very coarse'. Mainly for reasons of morale, neither alcohol nor cigarettes were rationed during the war, but their production was controlled and their availability was sometimes limited. 'Spirits were difficult to get', Marjorie Clowes recalls, but when her father did manage to obtain some 'the regulars got a quota'. Even goods that were rationed, such as coal, could sometimes be in short supply. In January 1945 the *Leicester Advertiser* reported that 'many householders' in Syston had been without coal for 'several days at a time. Some people are mixing coke with their supplies to make it last longer, and more fortunate people have wood to augment their supply'. In *Syston as I Remember It*, Irene Doig recalls that she and her brother used to 'have to go to Walker's Wood Yard with an old pram or wheelbarrow to collect logs to help the coal out. People used to go down the "Wash-Pit" [by the side of what later became the Memorial Playing Fields], and chop the trees down for firewood'. However, collecting firewood could be a pleasure as well as a necessity. Helen Cunliffe recalled 'sticking' expeditions, 'collecting fuel for the fire, and walking through a rough gate in the middle of the village… and being knee high in a field of buttercups'.

Economy Pattern for children's clothes.

Syston had an advantage, as many people already grew fruit and vegetables or kept hens. Les Pole's family had a large vegetable garden at the back of their house, where he 'helped reluctantly', and they also kept a pig 'down Bath Street (unofficially). When it was killed I remember we had half of it hanging in the bathroom. We shared it with Mr

Hamson, the greengrocer, who had a shop opposite our house on Leicester Road'. The Ministry of Food actively encouraged country dwellers to keep pigs to supplement their rations. Pig clubs were formed to pool resources in some parts of the country – though not in Syston - and 'pig bins' were sometimes placed in streets where householders could leave their kitchen waste to feed them. Talbott's the bakers in Bath Street kept pigs, and David Borderick's family, who lived at their shop on The Green, also had a pig sty in the big garden at the back of the shop. The pig was fed on table scraps, meal and items such as potato peelings, boiled up. They took their pig to be slaughtered at Annis's butcher's shop on High Street, between the Methodist Church and the Post Office, which had a small slaughter-house at the back. George Toon's father also kept a pig 'up Barkby Road in a small field next to The Limes, Miss Rice's house'.

A licence to slaughter a pig was required from the Food Office. As David Borderick also recalled: 'the pig owner had to take their ration book to the council office for some of their rations to be cancelled out' - but as Les Pole's reference to the 'unofficial' nature of their own pig suggests, this was not always observed. As desperately as the meat was needed, seeing a pig being killed could be an unpleasant experience for a child. Jennifer Turner (nee Hubbard) spent a lot of time at her grandparents' house in Bath Street during the war and 'once saw a pig being pole-axed from the upstairs window of the bakehouse... I remember it with horror even though it was over seventy years ago'. Margaret Hyman's father was a farmer at Barrow on Soar. They kept pigs for their own consumption and were allowed to kill two a year. She helped her mother to salt the meat afterwards to preserve it for bacon and ham: 'After the pig had been split into two halves these were laid in a very big flat salting tray, which was leaded at the bottom. The salt was in solid 7lb blocks, and we grated these, rubbed it into the meat, and then you had to totally cover the meat with it'. After the pig-killing Margaret's mother would sometimes make a pork pie as a treat. She also made brawn from the pig's head and cheeks, and 'the "pork fry" (that is the liver and kidney) was a special treat at this time'.

Ernest and Mary Gamble's wedding in September
1942 at Thurmaston Parish Church.
(Mary Gamble)

Meat rations were supplemented in other ways.
George Toon's family kept hens, and 'had a cockerel
in with them. It used to go for my mother every
time she went in the pen to fetch the eggs. So my
Dad killed it and we ate it!'. Helen Cunliffe's uncle
Lou [Louis] Wells had an iron foundry, J. and J.
Wells on Wellington Street, with 'a huge caged area
with dogs that I believe were used for retrieving
rabbits. Food was in such short supply that any
source was welcome and needed'. Michael Hall's
family kept rabbits in their garden for food. He used
to collect dandelion leaves for them on Millstone
Lane, on the edge of the village, but he and his
brother John also caught them in the wild: 'we would
sort of hypnotise the rabbit, and the other would
leap on top of it and grab it'. Not all the rabbits
eaten during the war came from such sources, as
Jennifer Turner remembers: 'My pet rabbit which I
loved disappeared near Christmas, and we had meat
that year'.

CLOTHES

Clothes were rationed from 1 June 1941 as production
was switched to supply demand for uniforms and
other essential war goods, and this continued until
March 1949. In 1942 the government introduced
a Utility clothing scheme to make new clothes
available at a controlled price, design and quality,
and clothing and shoe 'Exchanges' were also set up
by the Women's Voluntary Service (WVS) where
outgrown children's clothes could be changed for
others of a larger size. Mary Gamble was fortunate
enough to have her wedding and bridesmaids'
dresses specially made in 1942, thanks to the same
friend who helped with food for the reception. 'We
had only a small amount of coupons for clothes', as
she said:

> 'Our wonderful friend came to the rescue again.
> Auntie Evie, as we called her, knew the owner
> of a dress shop in Granby Street, and she was
> willing to let me have enough material, without
> coupons, to make my dress and two bridesmaids'
> dresses. Again, all illegal, so we had to keep quiet
> about how the material had been obtained. I was
> allowed seven yards of white moiré taffeta for
> my dress, and fourteen yards of turquoise taffeta
> for the bridesmaids, my two cousins'.

Mrs Drage, a neighbour who was also 'a very good
dressmaker', made the dresses, for a charge of £1,
sixpence extra for covered buttons and twopence
for sewing cotton. Betty Simpson recalled that her
own wedding 'finery' was 'only achieved by clothing
coupons donated by generous friends and family'.
However, a little ingenuity could go a long way
in obeying the government plea to 'make do and
mend', particularly in terms of wedding clothes.
Wedding dresses could be borrowed, or precious
coupons spent on an outfit that could be worn
again afterwards and made to look special with a
hat, corsage or other accessories. The same touches
might also be applied to a borrowed suit or dress.
Serving members of the Forces might be married
in uniform – and after the war men often wore the
'demob' suit of civilian clothes issued to them when
they were discharged.

7 WARTIME CHILDHOODS – EVACUEES, SCHOOLS AND FAMILY LIFE

EVACUEES

The evacuation of mothers and children from areas considered at high risk of bombing began on 1 September 1939, even before the declaration of war on Germany. Most of the evacuees who came to Syston at this time were from Sheffield, where the steel works were an obvious target for enemy action. On arrival by train at the Quorn and Woodhouse station, the children were examined by doctors and nurses before being sent by bus to Syston and other destinations including Barkby, Quorn, Sileby and Thrussington. Once in Syston, volunteers looked after them at the Assembly Rooms while they waited to be placed with local families. Over 30 of them also lived at Acacia House in School Street, long since demolished, opposite the school itself.

'Our visitors from Sheffield are comfortably settled in', the Syston parish magazine reported in October, paying tribute to the Billeting Officer, Mrs West,

'and her helpers for the efficient way this difficult bit of work has and is being carried out'. Initially anyone accommodating evacuees was paid 10s 6d for the first child and 8s 6d for each additional one; and if they could afford it, parents paid 6s a week per child to reimburse the government. The number of evacuees tended to fluctuate during the period of the 'Phoney War' up to June 1940, as some children returned home and others arrived, but the health of many was said to be improved by regular meals and a 'proper night's rest'. Praising those who had evacuees billeted with them for their 'forbearance and Christian charity', the Chairman of Leicestershire Education Committee, Sir Robert Martin, said in October 1939 that some 'had not seen a cooked meal in their lives. They did not know what to do with knives and forks. They were only accustomed to bread and butter and fish and chips, eaten on the front doorstep. The improvement in their physical appearance is already beyond belief'.

One of Syston's evacuees, Terry Riley of Bromley in Kent - third from the right celebrating VE Day with children of The Meadway. *(Michael Clarke)*

Acacia House, School Street, the home of Mrs Beatrice Hopcroft and her sister Miss Gertrude Harding, housed 30 evacuees during the war. *(Leicester Mercury Group)*

There were also concerns about evacuee children from towns moving into a rural environment. These 'inquisitive little guests', the National Safety First Association said in September 1939, lacked the knowledge acquired naturally by country children. They were at risk of picking 'strange berries' and trespassing in fields and woods protected by barbed wire. They were advised to avoid canals and rivers if unsupervised, and to learn to swim.

At least some of the Sheffield children were still in Syston in 1940. In October that year two of the girls were presented with fountain pens by the Syston Bowls Club 'in appreciation of help given during the season', and Les Pole recalled two girls from Sheffield being billeted with his family in St Peter's Street at this time. One woman whose family lived on The Meadway recalled that: 'We had a boy from Sheffield, Alan Peacock, with us, and there was another lad, Terry Riley, from London on The

Meadway'. Evacuees started to arrive from London from September 1940 as the German 'Blitz' began, and more came in 1944 when the V-1 flying bomb offensive was launched. 'We had two boys from Bromley, Kent billeted on us when we lived on the Leicester Road', Les remembers: 'They were Peter and Brian Jones. Peter was a teenager and was studying for his school certificate. He'd had to study in the shelter in Bromley as it was when the V1 bombs were being sent over'.

Among the evacuees recalled by Jennifer Turner were Cherie Nichols and her brother 'who stayed with Mr & Mrs Tizzard and their daughter Anne' on Fosse Way, and the Curry family who came from the London area and also lived on Fosse Way 'for the duration… Although they were older than me I played with them and we put on concerts to collect small sums of money to help the war effort'. Another evacuee and her son lived with Eileen

Freer and her family in Lower Church Street: 'She was Jamaican and her husband had been in the Air Force and had been killed when his plane was shot down. We called her Auntie Nelly and her son was called Donovan'. Joyce Brewerton came to the area with her family as an evacuee from Coventry during the bombing in 1940, finding refuge in Cossington. They stayed locally once the war was over, and Joyce lived all her married life on the Fosse Way in Syston. Jane Matthews' family also had evacuees from Coventry living with them – her mother's friend and her young family, whose house 'suffered considerable bomb damage. Just after the war I remember seeing all the windows boarded up and the bathroom wall in a heap on the hall floor'.

Empire Day Celebrations 1947 with a class of girls in the playground, and the office of Miss Berridge, the headmistress, on the right, showing the close proximity of Walker's woodyard to the school behind the girls.
(Jane Matthews)

WARTIME SCHOOLDAYS

The Syston parish magazine also noted in October 1940 that Queenie Holyoake, 'at one time Assistant Mistress in our Infants' School', had been evacuated to South Wales from Folkestone with some of her scholars. In Syston itself the arrival of evacuee children had an immediate impact on the village schools. Both the Infant and Junior Schools had recently received favourable reports from one of His Majesty's Inspectors. The Infant School was described as 'a good school... Both staff and children work hard and cheerfully to accomplish results of good standard... Free expression is also encouraged through Music and Dramatisation...'. The Inspector also commented 'very favourably on the high level of attainment and on the excellent

spirit' in the Junior School, and noted that the children 'take a pride in their appearance, have very pleasant manners, and put a great deal of effort into their work'. Even then, however, teaching conditions were 'difficult on account of lack of space', and as the numbers increased to well over 500 in September 1939 the schools soon became overcrowded.

The Minutes of meetings of the School Managers give a sense of the challenges they faced during the war, but the Log Books that recorded the day to day life of the schools have unfortunately disappeared. We have no details of the adjustments that had to be made to accommodate the extra children, nor any indication of just how many there were, but there are some hints from the Log Books of other nearby schools. For instance, the timetable at the Barkby Pochin School had to be reorganised to accommodate the 'incoming children from the city of Sheffield' – 21 of them in the Infants and Standard 1 by the end of September, alongside 37 Barkby children. Ten of the 72 children at Queniborough National School in the middle of that month were also evacuees, accompanied by one of the teachers from their Sheffield school. By April 1941, 130 of the 607 children on the roll at Roundhill Modern School were also evacuees.

Another matter of great concern was the safety of the children in the event of air raids during school hours. The Local Education Authority (LEA) advised that children living within a five minute walk could go home when a warning was sounded, but in Syston less than 25% fell into this category. In October 1939 the Parish Council sent a deputation to the County Council to press for air raid shelters at both schools. It was still awaiting them in September 1940, when it was claimed that 'after 12 months of threatened raids' the children 'had to rely on their desks for protection' in the case of urgent warnings. In March 1940 there were also complaints that windows fitted with special ARP meshing could no longer be opened or cleaned, and that sandbags were obstructing some of the drains.

Many local children attended Roundhill Modern School, opened in 1929, for their secondary education. Betty Toon was due to move to there in

Roundhill School – opened in 1929, this was the Secondary School for Syston children. *(Fisher & Potter)*

September 1939 for the new school year, but was unable to start until air raid shelters were provided later in the autumn. Until then, she recalled, 'teachers were sent out to take lessons with groups of children around the catchment area and keep in touch with pupils'. When they were finally able to attend the school they had to practise going down into the shelters when the bells and siren sounded the alarm. Tins of biscuits and buckets of water were taken down so they would have something to eat and drink while they waited for the 'All Clear'.

Some local children had to go further afield, either to grammar schools in Leicester or, in the case of Sybil Gamble (nee Marshall), to Barrow Grammar School where she had been awarded a scholarship. 'It was shortly after war was declared that I started school at Barrow', she remembers: 'the Autumn term started about two weeks late that year because the school had to have air raid shelters built on the school field. Some school rooms were also considered safe to use in the event of an air raid. Pupils at Barrow travelled from Syston by train, but because early morning trains were needed for

war-related work we caught the 10.30 train from Syston and left school at 3.30pm. We had lots of homework to do to make up for the short day at school'.

Maintaining an adequate number of teachers was difficult for all schools during the war, and as male teachers were called up for military service the LEA relaxed the rules requiring female teachers to give up their post on marriage. In June 1940 the School Managers in Syston approved Miss Watson's request to retain her position after her forthcoming marriage, as her husband would be in the army; and in July 1942 they dispensed with an interview when appointing Miss Doris Holyoake as an assistant mistress, as she was 'personally known' to most of them already. They were similarly supportive of the position of Mr W.H. Frost, a Conscientious Objector who taught in the Junior School and was a lay preacher at St Aidan's church. His offer to take up non-combatant duties had been rejected by the Tribunal that considered his application. Despite being instructed by the LEA that he 'could not be regarded as indispensible', the Managers considered it 'in the national interest' for him to remain in his present position until such time as his offer to join the Royal Army Medical Corps (RAMC) might be accepted as an alternative.

Their attitude contrasts with that of some members of the LEA itself. Among the 'strong views' expressed at a meeting in February 1941 was a resolution that 'it is against the public interest that anyone who refuses to fight in defence of the honour, liberty and lives of the people of this country should be in a position to teach the youth of the country'. In the view of one member, a Conscientious Objector teacher would be 'either looked up to or despised, and either reaction was dangerous to the country'. However, as another member reminded it, the Council had no powers to enforce its views. Decisions about individual cases were a matter for the Tribunals, and it should 'abide by the legislation and leave it at that'.

Playing in Central Park - Monica Naylor (nee Higgins), centre with her brother Michael, and cousin Shirley from Sheffield. *(Monica Naylor)*

The School Managers also had to deal with more mundane but equally pressing matters. In September 1941 the boiler in the Junior School was found to be in a 'highly dangerous condition' during an inspection: something that came as a 'great shock' to the Managers, 'whose chief concern is always the welfare and comfort of the children'. A '4000 shilling fund' was launched by Rev Tetley to raise the £200 needed to replace it, in the expectation that 'the warm-heartedness and generosity of the people of Syston' would rise to the challenge. Almost £60 had been raised by the end of 1941, but there is no record of the final total.

For the children themselves there were many lighter moments. Vivienne Everitt remembers an incident when she was in the top class in the Infants' School:

'although I was only six years old, my birthday being in July. Our teacher, Miss Berridge [who was also the Headmistress] had to go out of the room. She called me to the front of the class, handed me a piece of chalk and told me to write everyone's name on the board who talked when she was out of the room. This I did, and the more names I wrote down, the greater the uproar. I lost quite a few friends for a short time that day!'.

Margaret Thompson recalled a former teacher, Miss Sharp, who left to get married and later brought her baby into the school to show the children. Roundhill School also had an unexpected visit from a former mistress in June 1945, when Marguerite Henville (nee Davis) returned after an absence of seven years. She had been in Singapore with her husband Lawrence, and escaped the day before it fell in February 1942, spending the next three years in Australia. Her husband had stayed, and at this time was still a prisoner of the Japanese.

Children in the Junior School, where Mr Bowers was the Headmaster, were involved in various activities to help the war effort, and in March 1941 both boys and girls were reported to be knitting squares under the guidance of Miss Taylor, who then sewed them together to make blankets for the Red Cross. In *Syston as I Remember It*, Frank Astill recalled Mr Bowers giving the children:

'a lecture on not giving information to strangers concerning our area… I remember being in Mrs Greenfield's class in the junior school along with Percy Cooper, David Broughton, Eddie Scattergood, Guy Cherry, David Coddling, Ronnie Dennis, May Kirt, Ron Wayne, Adrian Cook, Josephine Bakewell and Harry Payne'.

Although Frank passed the Eleven Plus exam in 1944 and could have gone to a grammar school, he 'decided to go to Roundhill with Eddie Scattergood'. Mr Wakefield, Mr Veasey and Mrs Peabody – who taught technical drawing and also played the piano – were among the teachers he remembered from that time. Another memory was of spending fourteen school days from 8 am to 4 pm potato picking in August 1944, being taken to the fields on Pole's buses and earning 2s 6d a day.

Michael Hall experienced the more bureaucratic side of school life when his father Eric came home on leave. Eric worked for Midland Red buses before the war and joined the Royal Army Ordnance Corps (RAOC) four days before war was declared as he wanted to be an engineer. In 1940, after training, he was sent to Iceland where he remained for several years, only returning home twice on leave. On one of these occasions, when he was home for just five days, he kept his children off school so that he could spend all his available time with them. After the first day the School Board official who checked attendance called to find out why the children were not at school. Michael has a vivid memory of what happened next: Eric was so incensed that he grabbed the man by his lapels, lifted him up, and threw him over the privet hedge!

By 1944, as victory seemed finally within reach, education became a priority for post-war reconstruction. The main focus of the Education Act of that year was on secondary education, but it also had implications for 'aided' schools such as those in Syston: state-funded but with the Church having a substantial influence in their running. The Managers were anxious that the schools retained this status 'as a point of honour for the diocese', while recognising that 'possibly half' the population of Syston was Nonconformist in religion, and a substantial number of parents 'may be inclined to argue that since the schools are to be Church Schools, churchmen should find the money for them'.

Whoever paid for them, it was clear that new schools would eventually be needed. As the war continued the buildings deteriorated due to their age and lack of upkeep. In June 1944 the Managers described both schools as 'inadequate', and they 'will be more so after the war' in the light of a Parish Council application for 380 new houses to be built. In January 1945 the Infant School was damaged by a fire at the nearby timber yard of George Walker, and by March that year the

Managers were describing it as 'disgraceful and totally inadequate and out-of-date'. The work of the school was constantly disrupted by the sawmill next door: and 'the noise is getting on the nerves of the children and teachers. There are 47 children in one classroom, and the only entrance is through another classroom'. Soon afterwards they concluded that it was 'impossible' to bring the Infant School up to a reasonable standard, and decided to transfer the children to the Junior School, until the site adjacent to the church on Upper Church Street, already earmarked for a new Junior School, could be utilised.

Christmas card to Anne and Jack Evatt from their father, Christmas 1944

As the School Managers had predicted, the demand for school accommodation increased as the post-war population of Syston itself grew. Various halls were used as extra classrooms, including the Parish Rooms on Broad Street, the Primitive Methodist School Room on Melton Road, the Assembly Rooms, and the Day Nursery on Leicester Road. In 1954 a new three classroom block was built on

Upper Church Street. A new Junior School was built close to this in 1964 and occupied in the following year. The Infant School remained in High Street, and the three classes using outside halls moved into the School Street buildings. It closed in 1972, but the last Infant classes only moved from School Street to Upper Church Street in September 1976.

MEMORIES OF FAMILY LIFE

Many of the people that were interviewed for this book were children during the war. Their memories often offer a different perspective on its effects, particularly on family life when a parent was away from home for long periods or worked very long hours. Monica Naylor 'hardly ever saw my Dad. He worked long hours in Leicester during the day and he was in charge of the local AFS unit'. Doreen Payne, who was living in Thurmaston at the time, recalled that her father worked very long hours at the British United factory on Belgrave Road in Leicester, 'where he was employed making munitions for the war effort. He worked all night from 7 pm until 7 am the following day, and at the height of the war he worked for seven nights every week'. Jennifer Turner's father served all over the country with the National Fire Service, and when he came home on one occasion for a 24 hour break 'he changed from his uniform into civvies and I cried and wondered who this strange man was'. Eileen Freer's family lived in Lower Church Street just off the Green:

'There was Norman (my older brother), me, and Veronica (my younger sister) who slept in Mum's and Dad's room. While Dad was away Veronica slept with Mum. When Dad returned from the war Veronica would not accept that this man was her Dad as her Dad was that picture that stood on the sideboard, and she was not happy that this man had come and taken her place in the bed. She had to come in with me as Mum said it was Dad and it was his bed!'.

Many people lived in cramped conditions during the war as families had to share accommodation for various reasons. Vivienne Everitt remembers living with her grandparents in Thurmaston from 1939 until 1943: 'After Grandma died in 1942, in our

small house were my Mum, me, my baby brother Chris, along with my aunt, my cousin Rosemary, my Grandpa, and Freda and Colin Whittaker'. To a small child this seemed normal at the time, but looking back on it: 'Goodness knows where we all slept, let alone sat down for a meal'.

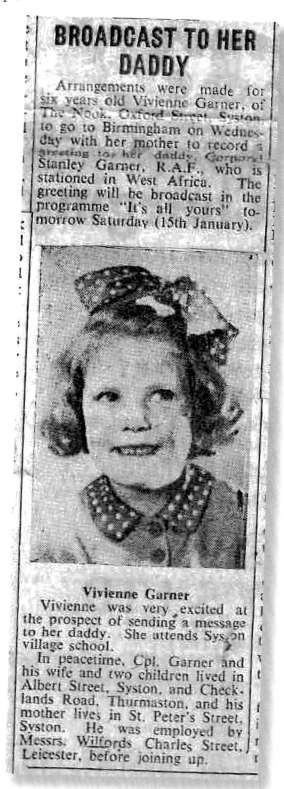

Newspaper Cutting – Vivienne Garner recording a message to her father in West Africa, January 1944.
(Syston and District Times)

Families did exchange letters with loved ones away from home, of course, but these could take a very long time to arrive, particularly from overseas. Vivienne recalled that: 'Once I landed up in Groby Road isolation hospital with the measles. My Dad received a letter from Mum saying I was out of hospital, but he had never received the letter telling him why I went in!'. Later in the war Vivienne had the chance to record a message for her father, Corporal Stanley Garner, who was serving in West Africa with the RAF:

'In December 1943 Mum had a letter from the BBC asking if a child from our family would like to record a message for "It's All Yours", a programme which was going to be broadcast on 15th January to West Africa. We had to go to Birmingham on January 12th to record the message. I was the only child without my message written down. I remember that the producer was quite stressed out because he thought I would freeze when it was time for me to speak, but not me! We sat about eight of us at a round table with a huge microphone, and all went well. When the broadcast went out I was allowed to stay up late to listen to the programme, and I was also on the featured on the front page of the *Syston Times*'.

This sort of contact became still more important for morale on both sides as the war continued, and there were similar broadcasts to other parts of the world. In May 1944 the *Leicester Evening Mail* reported that Mrs E. Hubbard of Syston 'will travel to London on Tuesday with her two little boys Graham and David to send live greetings over the radio in the programme "Hello Gibraltar" to her husband Hector Hubbard of the RAF'. In peacetime, the newspaper noted, Mr Hubbard was a batsman for Syston Town Cricket Club, and a foreman at Johnson and Barnes, Rutland Street, Leicester. His parents lived at Thurmaston, and his father had been an umpire for Thurmaston Town Cricket Club 'for many seasons'.

Christmas could be a difficult time for families who were separated, or because of shortages of food and other items. Monica Naylor's first memory of Christmas was in 1939, when she was nearly three.

She remembers:

'lying in a darkened bedroom suffering from measles, when Father Christmas arrived, presumably a dressed up fireman. Christmas toys were homemade. My Sheffield grandmother (not really into knitting) knitted a teddy for me in khaki wool which had shoe-button eyes. Mother made it a "posh suit" in recycled green velvet'.

Later in the war, when toys were very difficult to get, Monica's parents did a 'make do and mend' present for her: 'One year a doll appeared with white legs and arms which I quickly recognised as the limbs of a doll whose head had got broken. A new head from the dolls' hospital, and a nice outfit were supposed to fool me!'. Their family Christmas was celebrated 'very quietly' during the war:

'no noisy games allowed. The small artificial tree went up on Christmas Eve, not before. We always had a cockerel for dinner, which I didn't like, but Gran, who was a brilliant player at Whist always used to win one, then at the next Whist Drive would usually win a rabbit for me. We had a homemade Christmas pudding with silver 3d pieces in it, magic I thought!'.

Jennifer Turner made paper cards and decorative chains out of wallpaper scraps for Christmas, and 'we had a feather Christmas tree'. Jane Marshall's mother bought her a Christmas tree from a shop in the village: 'and when we walked home the Misses Hayward, who lived in Holmdale Road, saw us. The next day they brought us a box of beautiful Christmas decorations for the tree. It is one of the kindest things I remember and I treasured these decorations for many years'. Joan Quinn's only memory of Christmas at that time was:

'going to Grandma's next door. My Granddad would dress up as Father Christmas and there would be a small present on the tree for each of us which he would give out. We only ever got a couple of presents in our sack with a few nuts and an orange if we were lucky'.

Christine Sanderson remembered 'always going to Nana's for tea on Christmas Day with all the family,

Evacuee card game – four cards from the pack.

and doing our "piece" in the front room to entertain the gathering'. Eileen Freer:

'didn't have any toys that I remember, but what I do remember is that us kids used to turn the dining room table upside down and we had many adventures playing pirates and the table was a ship. At Christmas we always had an orange, an apple and some nuts in our stockings, but I cannot remember any toys'.

At other times of the year the radio and cinema were important sources of entertainment as well as news and information. Jean Sykes remembered that: 'We had music on the wireless on Sunday evenings while Mum and I did sewing'. They also played cards and board games, and listened to *Dick Barton, Special Agent*, a very popular radio serial. Monica Naylor used to attend the Saturday Matinee at the Savoy cinema: '3d for children. I liked going'. She always 'had to rush out at the end' to help in the family grocery shop on Leicester Road, 'where there would be a queue of kids wanting to buy natural liquorice (wooden sticks) which you could buy without ration coupons'. Frank Astill, who was born in Syston in 1931 and lived in Central Avenue, also wrote in *Syston as I Remember It* of standing outside the Savoy Cinema in Syston on a Friday night: 'if it was an "A" film you had to ask someone to take you in. Mr Roughton, the manager, was very strict'.

Frank earned some money while still at school by doing a paper round for Peberday's newsagents':

'My round was the Avenues. I used to deliver 95 in the morning at 6.30 am and 112 at night, from Mrs Dalley's to Millstone Lane. Saturday evening we would also collect the week's paper money from most people. Then we were each sent in turn to Mr Peberday to total up and get our 5s 6d wages'.

Some sights were memorable because of their strangeness or rarity for a child. 'I was bathed in the kitchen sink at night', Jane Matthews (nee Talbott) recalled: 'and could never understand why two large sheets of plywood were put over the windows when it got dark. It was of course part of the blackout procedure, but much to my mother's annoyance, I would keep fiddling with the wing nut that held them in place, so there were a few dodgy moments'. She also clearly recalls:

'seeing my father [Walter Talbott] leave Leicester Midland Station to set sail for the Far East. My mother stood on the station steps leading down to the platform with me in her arms and we looked down on a sea of soldiers waiting to board the train. I distinctly remember how crowded and noisy it was'.

One woman who lived in The Meadway during the

war remembers seeing large convoys of American troops going through the village, and on one occasion:

> 'Mother got us up in the night once to see the sky full of parachutes [looking towards Barkby]. We saw another large parachute drop in the morning on the way to school. Presumably these were practice runs for Arnhem or D-Day, although we didn't know that at the time'.

Inevitably some children were affected personally by the death of a relative or friend of the family. Christine Sanderson vividly remembers the day she heard that her next door neighbour and honorary 'Uncle' Walter Talbott, who was in the Air Force, had been killed. She recalled 'how terrible it was when Aunty Lydia came round with the news that he had been killed. I can still see her sitting in our back room. Their daughter Jane stayed with us that night'.

8 OVER HERE – US FORCES AND ITALIAN AND GERMAN PRISONERS OF WAR

AMERICAN TROOPS AROUND SYSTON

The first American troops arrived in Britain in January 1942, in anticipation of an eventual invasion of mainland Europe. The nearest base to Syston was the US War Department Services of Supply depot established at Ashby Folville near Melton in November 1942, which stored tons of ammunition and supplies for airfields of the US 8th Army Air Force (USAAF). This had a satellite camp at Gaddesby, and in June 1943 both were taken over by the USAAF and re-designated Air Force Station 520. Until May 1945 this was the base for a succession of 'Quartermaster Truck' units consisting mainly of Black Americans. In the official US language of the time they were 'colored', something which Helen Cunliffe found confusing as a child: 'My mother said I must be prepared for coloured soldiers coming from America. I was so disappointed when they turned out to be brown. I had been imagining all colours of the rainbow!'.

Despite the inevitable problems caused by the arrival of large numbers of US troops in Leicestershire in the summer of 1944, they were generally received with 'kindness'. In a letter to Sir Arthur Hazlerigg in June that year, a US Major-General asked him to pass on the 'grateful appreciation we all feel for the generous, sympathetic and hospitable reception' accorded to them:

> 'The cordial manner in which my officers and troops were received upon their arrival, the sympathetic attitude with which their presence was viewed, and in the light of which the many problems they have created have been solved, are jointly a source of admiration for your peoples and a stimulus to effort on our part to broaden and strengthen the understanding friendships which have such a great future potential for us both'.

The social life of Syston was certainly enlivened by US soldiers in the locality. Dot Wilkes recalled that servicemen stationed at Gaddesby added to the numbers for the 'well patronised' dances held 'by courtesy of Mr Whitelaw at the Assembly Rooms next to the cinema'. In *Syston as I Remember It*, Frank Astill recalled 'the Yanks' as particularly liking the Fox and the Bell pubs, the latter being 'very lively' on a Saturday evening. There was clearly some contact as well with USAAF bases in Rutland, as two Syston women married servicemen from units stationed there. On 16 December 1944 Helene Tetley (17), the eldest daughter of Syston's vicar, Rev F.B. Tetley, married Major Alfred Camden Cromartie (28) of Garland, North Carolina, in the parish church. He was based at USAAF Station 493 at Harringworth near Uppingham with the 315th Troop Carrier Group of the 9th Army Air Force - whose C47 Dakotas towed gliders carrying British, American and Polish paratroops during the Normandy landings in June 1944 and later operations in Europe. 'The bells of St. Peter's, Syston, "rang in" the bride…', the *Leicester Evening Mail* reported on the day of the wedding:

Wartime Wedding – an unknown US Serviceman and his bride leaving St Peter and St Paul's Church.

57

'Col. A.L. Holtz and Col. H.B. Lyons, of the USAAF, and 10 brother officers of the bridegroom were among the guests. The bridesmaids were Miss Joan Castle, Miss Kathleen Castle, Miss June Preston and Miss Elizabeth Rudd, who wore pink taffeta dresses with heart-shaped necks, sashes and full skirts, and headdresses of tulle net. Capt. E. Rice was best man, and the groomsmen were Lieut. W.F. McArthy, USAAF, Mr. W.H. Frost and Mr. Godfrey Tetley...'.

The bride – popularly known as 'Paddy' - wore a satin gown with seed pearl embroidery and headdress, an accordion-pleated train and long tulle veil, and carried an ivory prayer book. The reception at the Church Hall in Syston was attended by 130 guests, strongly suggesting a helping hand from the Americans with the catering. Helene and Alfred's eldest son, Ian Camden Cromartie, was born in Leicester in January 1946. Alfred Cromartie later became a Colonel in the United States Air Force, and is buried in Arlington National Cemetery near Washington DC.

Olive Gunby, who lived in High Street, married Ernest Howard Chambers in April 1945. He was serving with the 316th Troop Carrier Group at USAAF Station 489 at Cottesmore, near Oakham. Both were 23 when they married. The War Brides Act of December 1945 enabled US servicemen to bring their 'alien' brides and children into the country without the usual restrictions on immigration, and in January 1946 Olive left for the USA on the ship *Argentina* with her three month old daughter Susan to join her husband, a 1st Lieutenant in the US Army. Other Syston 'War Brides' included Peggy (Ilene) Marshall (18), the daughter of the Syston haulage contractor John Marshall of Barkby Road, who married Michael James Smith of the USAAF on 3 February 1945. His home was in Wadsworth, Ohio and he was based at Harborne Park in Smethwick, Birmingham at the time. Peggy and Michael's son Andrew James Smith was born in December 1945 and baptised at Syston in March 1946. On 3 November 1945 Margaret Crump (18) married William Jack Aho, who was based at USAAF Station 520 at Ashby Folville. Margaret

lived in Sandford Road and her occupation is given in the Syston marriage register as a clerk.

Other marriages to US servicemen can occasionally be found in newspaper reports, like that of Joan Marjery Tompkins (25) who married Sergeant Stanley G. Janson of the USAAF in Suffolk in February 1945. She was the eldest daughter of the late F.W. Tompkins, former Stationmaster at Saxby, and Mrs Tompkins, of 'The Elms', Leicester Road, Syston. Wearing a gown of white satin with a full length train and headdress of orange blossom and carrying a bouquet of white carnations, she was given away by her mother. In March 1946 Joan left Southampton on the *Christobal* for her new home in Detroit with her eight month old son Cedric W. Janson. Mary Teresa Smith (22), the daughter of Arthur and Beatrice Smith of Syston, was married to James Joseph Hahnenburg of the US forces in April 1945 and sailed from Southampton two years later with her eldest son Adrian James, who was born in April 1946.

The arrival of the US troops brought much extra traffic to Syston, sometimes with tragic consequences. On 12 August 1944 the *Leicester Advertiser* reported the death of Kenneth Whitehead, age 4, of Melton Road, after a collision with a US Army vehicle. Kenneth had four older siblings and three younger ones, and their father was serving overseas with the Leicestershire Regiment at the time. His elder brother Tony remembers that:

'We were playing under the Brook bridge, and Kenneth dashed out and was knocked down and killed by a US army jeep with two soldiers in. Grandma lived in the Brook cottages, and we'd gone up to her house, but she said she was too busy to have us there that day. So we were going back home, and stopped to play under the bridge which we often did. We were almost like twins, and we'd swapped our jumpers over. So when someone rushed up home to tell Mum about the accident there was some confusion about which one of us had been knocked over'.

The US troops in the area of Syston were remembered for many years after the war, but one of their legacies was not discovered until 70 years after it ended when workmen excavating a car park on the Barkby Road industrial estate uncovered a World War II shell. The site was previously used for target practice by US troops, and as 92-year old Ken West told the *Leicester Mercury* on 27 July 2015: 'For years after the war young lads used to go up there looking for souvenirs. One or two walked home with live ammunition'. The same article quoted another *Mercury* reader who had previously related his own 'boyhood adventures' on the site, where he found buried bazooka shells with their fins on 'and wires sticking out. We tried to ignite them by throwing them at rocks – but we didn't realise we needed a battery, so nothing happened. We were lucky – I don't know what would have happened if one had gone off'.

Italian Prisoners of War at the War Memorial.
(George Toon)

ITALIAN AND GERMAN PRISONERS OF WAR

The first Italian Prisoners of War (POWs) were brought to Britain from July 1941 after being captured in the Middle East. In January 1942 the government decided to make use of them to supplement the agricultural labour force, allowing those of 'good conduct' to live in on farms or in

hostels 'from which they will be available for employment by neighbouring farmers'. Camps were set up to house them as their numbers increased following the Italian surrender in 1943, including that on Barkby Lane on the site of a former Heavy Anti-aircraft (HAA) Battery. Unlike the German POWs brought to Britain from the summer of 1944 following the invasion of Normandy, Italians who volunteered to work in agriculture as 'co-operators' enjoyed considerable freedom, and often found a place in the local community. Along with American servicemen stationed in the area, Italian POWs attended Roman Catholic services in the Syston Assembly Rooms, conducted by members of the Rosminian Order from Ratcliffe College; and in December 1944 around 30 of them performed an opera, *Dr Saori* (composer unknown), at the Rooms before 'a crowded audience', raising £9 from a collection in aid of the fund to build a Catholic church in the village. On the other hand, not all local people were inclined to be friendly to the local POWs. Grace Berrington, who was 15 when the war started, 'never went anywhere near them. My Dad would have killed me'.

German Prisoners of War from the Barkby Lane camp were also employed locally, among them two known as Ferdie and Fritz who worked for J. Shuttlewood and Son on Barkby Road, Syston. Molly Toon, the youngest member of the family, recalled that: 'Every day my mother – the farmer's wife – cooked enough dinner for me to take the POWs, hearty helpings served in two large basins. These comprised of meat and vegetables from the farm plus a pudding or pie made with homegrown fruit' (*Leicester Mercury*, 4 July 1995). Local children remember the Italians making rings for them from sixpenny pieces, and German POWs carving toys or other items from wood. From Christmas 1946 German POWs were allowed to visit British homes, but friendships developed earlier in spite of regulations. In October 1946 a woman from Queniborough pleaded guilty to sending a letter to a German POW at the Barkby Lane camp 'without lawful authority', having met him while working at an Ordnance Depot where a number of German POWs were employed. This came to light following the escape of four POWs from the camp in August that year, during an inspection of the kit of two who returned voluntarily. She admitted being 'very foolish' – 'I knew I was doing wrong from the beginning' - but felt sorry for him after receiving a letter 'in which he told her of his hardships'. Fining her £1, the Chairman of the Magistrates concluded that: 'It might have been quite innocent on her part, and he had no doubt that this would be a lesson to her'.

Once the war ended, former POWs were often employed in work such as road-building as well as agriculture while awaiting repatriation. Near to Syston, this included a 16 inch wide path laid across the fields from Barkby Thorpe/Hamilton Road to the house of the Tomlinson family in Barkby. 'Although it was better than the mud track', Les and Tony Tomlinson recalled in a family history, 'balance was important or you ended up in a ploughed furrow'. The last 250 German prisoners did not leave Leicestershire until November 1948. 'Despair and tears were in evidence at London Road Station, Leicester, today', the *Leicester Mercury* reported on their departure: 'as sweethearts said farewell to their German farmworker friends… A considerable element of these civilianised Germans are reluctant to leave the farms, food and friends in Leicestershire to go back to a country where the rigours of winter have now begun'.

9 AWAY AT THE WAR – SYSTON MEN AND WOMEN IN HM FORCES

LETTERS HOME

News of at least some of the Syston men and women serving in the forces during the war can be gleaned from newspapers or sources such as the parish magazine. There are very few detailed personal accounts, and those that do exist are all the more valuable for having survived. Among them are letters sent by Geoff Meadows to his wife Nora (nee Taylor). The extracts reproduced here by permission of his daughter Joy Lambell give a real insight into Geoff's wartime experiences and the importance of this kind of contact during a very long period of separation.

Geoff was a gunner in the Royal Artillery and joined the Army in July 1939. In March 1940 he was sent to France and evacuated from Dunkirk at the end of May on a paddle steamer. Geoff and Nora were married at Syston parish church by special licence on 18 June 1940, when he was home on leave for four days. He was 20 and she was 19. 'Money was tight', as Joy says: 'so Mum carried a prayer book instead of flowers. She always wished she had been able to afford flowers'. In August 1941 Geoff sailed for India, stopping off for three days in Cape Town on the way. By then Nora was expecting their first child, Ann, who was born in February 1942. A cable was received towards the end of October to say that he had arrived safely, and soon afterwards he was promoted to Sergeant. He wrote home in December from his base on the North West Frontier, after receiving eight letters from Nora on the same day - all written in the last week of August and first week of September. It was 'a heavenly surprise to get eight at once like that', he wrote in reply, before describing a recent journey with a convoy:

'I was put in charge of a convoy of 3 ton lorries that had to go to the ordnance depot at Rawalpindi. It's a two and a half day journey by road from here through tribal territory. I drove one of the lorries all the way there and I really enjoyed it although I was a bit tired when I arrived. Of course we had to have armoured cars and troops as escort through the worst part of the tribal country, but parts of the countryside were in themselves worth making the trip for, they were really marvellous. At one place – the Kohat Pass - there is a five mile climb up the mountains, the road is very narrow going up and on one side there is a sheer drop of thousands of feet and on the other side a sheer climb of a few more thousand feet. There were also dozens of blind corners so you can imagine how careful we had to be. When we got to the top though there was a wonderful panorama of the plains and on looking down we could see the end of the convoy winding up the mountain pass several thousand feet below. The temperature was at freezing point at the top by the way'.

Dot Wilkes (standing) and fellow WAAFs by a staff car. *(Dot Wilkes)*

In January 1942, just before Geoff left India for the Middle East, he wrote to Nora: 'Tell [your] Dad we can't get any beer at all now so you can imagine how we enjoy ourselves in the evening, the wireless is our only comfort'. In Cyprus in May 1942 he received a letter written by Nora the previous December, asking him to wire the name he would like for their baby. This had been to India before it caught up with him, only adding to the loneliness of separation. 'I know what loneliness is like', he wrote in March 1944:

'how it plays on your nerves until you feel you will go mad. I feel more and more like that every day... just the same cold rain and mud and wet clothes to work in... the same truck to sit in night after night with nothing to read. It all gets you down after a time and makes you very restless, that's why some nights I just can't settle down to write to you...'.

Later that month he was greatly cheered by receiving a photograph of Nora and Ann, who was then two years old: 'the most wonderful picture I have ever seen in my life... you have no idea how that photograph has cheered me up. I just can't keep my eyes off it'. Geoff eventually met Ann in July 1944 when he was home for ten weeks' leave, having been away for almost three years.

LONG SEPARATIONS

Such long separations were not unusual. Mary Timson lived in Thurmaston during the war and moved to Syston in 1961. She married Ernest Gamble at Thurmaston parish church in September 1942, and he was called up at the end of 1943. Ernest joined the Lincolnshire Regiment, and after training in England and Ireland he was sent firstly to India and then to 'jungle school' on Camilla Island, off Southern India. From there his unit was sent to Burma and Imphal in North East India, and then to fight the Japanese in Sumatra in 1945. Knowing of the Japanese reputation for cruel treatment of prisoners, Mary was 'terrified in case he got captured. I felt a real dread and helplessness, but there was nothing I could do'. Keeping in touch was very difficult. 'They were not proper letters', she remembers: 'They were airmail letters that were censored if you used your own words'. Like all soldiers, Ernest had to choose from a list of suggested phrases as a security measure.

Even after the Japanese surrender in August 1945 the war was not over for many British soldiers in the Far East. There were still pockets of resistance in the jungle areas of Sumatra and Borneo, and Mary was not to see Ernest again until March 1947. When he finally came home, she had just

a couple of hours notice with a phone call, as he 'wasn't allowed to tell me he was on his way'. As the *Leicester Advertiser* reported on 1 April 1944, the wife of Signalman Walter Bailey-Taynton of Mostyn Avenue had no notice at all of his return until she was awakened by a knocking on her window at 3 am. He had been serving with the 8th Army in North Africa and Gibraltar, and she and her three year old daughter had not seen him for nearly three years. In August 1945 the *Advertiser* also reported the return of Private Ernest Whitehead of Melton Road, who had been away for three years. While fighting with the Leicestershire Regiment in the 14th Army against the Japanese in Burma he had taken part in a 500 mile trek under the command of Major Geoffrey Lockett MC, in monsoon weather through 'some of the worst country on Northern Burma', to take control of the Kyusanlai Pass, a key route to a British garrison. They were 'never dry', he told the newspaper, and often had to 'slog along' waist deep in water, with leeches clinging to them. 'It was a fallacy that the Japs were all short men', he added: 'He had seen many 6 ft in height and very well built. They were reckless... and didn't mind dying'.

Ernest's brother Stanley was serving in Burma at the same time, and 'by coincidence', the *Advertiser* reported, came out of the jungle as Ernest went in. They had tried to meet at a jungle airstrip, but 'Stan landed at No. 74 strip by mistake, instead of No. 47, and they did not meet'. Ernest did meet a fellow Systonian in Burma, Wilfred Hawkins, who had worked as a conductor for the Midland Red bus company before the war; and the *Advertiser* reported several other chance meetings between men away on active service. In India late in 1943, 'quite by accident', Corporal H.G.R. Sharpe (RAFVR), whose mother lived in Goodes Lane, discovered that he was camped just a few miles away from Sergeant Jack Allen of School Street. Both were employed by the LMS railway in Leicester in peacetime. Around the same time Sergeant Harry Walton of Barkby Road and Private Harry (Stormer) Branson of Lower Church Street also met by chance while serving in North Africa. In civilian life Sergeant Walton was a painter and a member of the Wreake Angling Club, while

Extract from Geoff Meadow's letter to his wife Nora, written in January 1941.

Private Branson, a boot and shoe operative, was a 'prominent' member of Syston St Peter's football club. Driver William Byatt (RASC) of Brookside and Driver Alan Creasey (RAOC) of Millstone Lane also managed to get together in Egypt after 'trying to meet for many months', as the *Leicester Mercury* reported in December 1943. 'We had 48 hours together', Driver Byatt wrote to his parents:

'and what a time we had! We are to meet again after Christmas'.

Syston men and women also feature in reports of awards for bravery. In December 1944 Flying Officer Allan George Sheffield RAFVR, son of Mr and Mrs George Sheffield of High Street, was awarded the Distinguished Flying Cross (DFC) for 'the utmost courage and devotion to duty in numerous operations against the enemy'. He had worked in his father's butchery business before volunteering for service in the RAF in 1940, serving first in Fighter Command and transferring to Bomber Command in 1943 when he took part in 31 sorties over Germany and occupied territory. He received his commission in 1944. Both his brother and sister also served in the RAF during the war. In September 1945 Pauline Sutliff, daughter of Mr and Mrs Charles Sutliff of Goodes Lane, also received an award for 'devotion to duty'. As a telephone operator, she was attached to the ATS in its London control room throughout the London Blitz, and 'had some hectic experiences', the *Leicester Advertiser* reported:

'bombs and doodle-bugs dropping all around… Once, when in the control room during a temporary lull the officer in charge suggested some coffee. One of the girls went to prepare it, and was going back into the room when there was a terrific blast from a doodle-bug and all her clothes were torn off'.

Charles Lowe in Egypt. He served in World War 1 and was a member of the Home Guard until he was called up in 1943. He then served with the Royal Electrical and Mechanical Engineers.

BETTY SIMPSON'S WARTIME MEMORIES

Betty Goodwill and Bert Simpson met in Syston in 1940 and were married at the parish church on 23 August 1941, when Bert was serving in the Military Police. Many years later their daughter Val Fairburn wrote that:

'My father Bert Simpson was lucky to be sent to Broad Street in Syston to recover after being in action at Dunkirk in the early part of the Second World War. He felt lucky for two reasons. [Firstly], when he volunteered to train as a pilot he might have been sent to Canada. Many of his friends died there as they often had to fly solo before they were fully trained. [Secondly], my mother, then Betty Goodwill, lived in Broad Street! The story told by Bert was that Betty was out walking and pushed her little Terrier dog Peggy into a ditch. Bert, who was on crossroad duty, being a perfect gentleman, rescued the dog. Mum always hotly denied that the dog was pushed! Betty had lots of suitors but she fell in love with Bert. Like many others during the war they decided to marry as soon as possible.

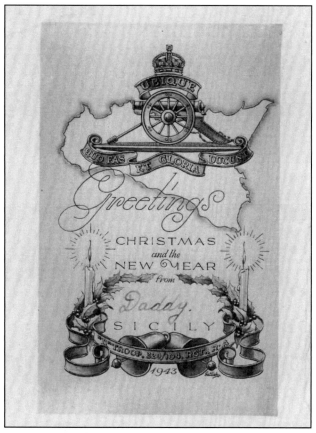

Christmas card to Mary, Joan and Guy Cherry from their father George Cherry, December 1943.

Several decades ago Betty wrote her own memories of the war, along with a poem about her feelings on seeing troops depart for Arnhem. Val has kindly given her permission to reproduce them here:

'The title "wartime memories" revives so many experiences that it is hard to make a choice! Part

Bert and Betty Simpson's wedding, August 1941. *(Val Fairbaim).*

of this should be my wartime wedding, the finery only achieved by clothing coupons donated by generous friends and family. I was mainly hidden, anyway, by my enormous bouquet of roses, donated by the local rose grower. .. My unforgettable memory must, however, be the September morning in 1944 when we heard the drone of a fleet of aircraft towing their amazing cumbersome gliders to "who knew where?". It was sunny and still as only an English Sunday morning can be, until disturbed by this persistent, penetrating hum. I had been expecting some important operation as my glider-pilot husband had been denied any leave, and it was obvious that tension was mounting. We soon knew that Arnhem was the target - the operation intended to drastically shorten the war. Very soon, glued to the radio, I became frantically worried as all was obviously not going according to plan and the fighting became desperate with no relief.

'Hitler's Panzer's Divisions were unexpectedly reinforcing Germany's other troops there and then the First Airborne Division was trapped. Hopelessly outnumbered, they fought with courage and endurance, while at home the reports became increasingly terrifying. When it was finally over and I learned that only 2,000 out of the original 10,000 had got back, my anxiety was overwhelming. I was desperate to know what had happened to my husband, and as soon as the wounded began to trickle back I went round all the hospitals trying to get a glimpse of hope. The scenes were appalling: some were to encourage me, others gave reason to despair though all [those I spoke to] were amazingly kind.

'The days passed with no word and time hinged on the postman who passed week after week.. My young baby really kept me going but time seemed endless. Months went by with no news and eventually the authorities told me that I would have to go on "Widow's Pension" if no word came. Then the marvellous morning arrived when a dog-eared card arrived saying that my husband was "wounded and a P.O.W". The relief was indescribable and it was to be a long, long time before I was to know why I had heard nothing. After being slightly wounded he had escaped capture from the Germans and after days in the fields, travelling by night and existing on turnips and swedes, he contacted an isolated farm whose occupants found him when the hay in the barn was observed to move. They put him in touch with the wonderful and heroic Dutch underground who fed him and moved him from one site to another. I heard of the brave housewife who found a German knocking at her door while my husband hovered behind it with a carving knife to hand; the schoolmaster's loft and the excursions on a bike for exercise at night, dressed in the local policeman's uniform! [I heard also of the] later recapture and the jump off the train to freedom again having cut through the lock of the cattle wagon. Two more men jumped with him as the train slowed round a bend and tragically one was shot, the bullets missing my husband as he rolled down a bank.

'Once more he was eventually helped by the underground and spent much time in dugouts, sharing with others of various nationalities. They got to know each other extraordinarily well, needless to say, and my husband remembers Dickens' *Tale of Two Cities* being passed around to be read by precious candle-light. The final escape attempt was foiled by a German patrol and this time they cited him as a possible spy and put him in solitary confinement with constant interrogation. Eventually they transported him far away to a prison camp on the Polish border. When the Russians advanced the inmates were driven out by their German captors to face the horrendous 200 mile trek in 20 degrees below zero to yet another P.O.W. camp. So many died on the way from cold and starvation that I still feel so very fortunate that my husband's "nine lives" were still not used up. A friend and he walked out in the chaos of the German defeat before the Russians had taken complete charge, and an American jeep picked up two thin and bedraggled allies and arranged a flight back to "dear old England".

'After all these months and the one solitary card, I received a wonderful phone call one day to simply say "I am back". The best day of my life, I'm sure, and forty five years later I am so thankful to be fortunate enough to "tell the tale". This is, of course, only a small part of it and I guess I will never know it all, for it has only come out "in bits" over the years. The happy sequel to all is the wonderful friendship built up through the years with those brave Dutch families who hid my husband at the risk of their own lives.

Our many post-war pilgrimages to Arnhem have reinforced these very special links that will never be broken'.

ARNHEM LIFT

A Sunday morning, bright and clear
  In autumn's misty glow,
The sound of droning aircraft
  Disturbs the quiet below.

The powered aircraft's pulsing hum,
  The Gliders towed behind,
A sight so wondrous, fearful too,
  Whose mission secrets bind.

How could we know these brave young men
  With courage in that hour,
Turned to Commandos when cast off,
  And landed without power!

No-one could know the hope sustained,
  Would Arnhem end the war?
And if not, how could they be risked?
  The hopes of all could soar.

'Twas not to be, though gallantly
  They faced the Panzer's might,
Enduring more than humans should
  They stood alone to fight.

So few came back, much eager youth
  Was lost on Holland's shore,
I always hoped, my pilot DID
  Return to me once more!

Betty Simpson

Able Seaman Robert Wright who died in France aged 18 three days after D-day when his landing craft was hit by shell fire. Less than a year before he was one of the youngest members of Syston Home Guard.

PRISONERS OF WAR

Some local families waited months or even years for news of men posted missing or taken prisoner. Driver Edward Stanley Bates (33) of the Royal Army Service Corps (RAOC), and a member of the Syston Salvation Army, was reported missing in the Middle East in April 1941. It was not until September that year that his wife and mother in Syston received a letter to say that he was a prisoner of the Germans in Stalag XVIIIa, near Wolfsberg in Austria. He was 'in good health', he said: 'and in a good camp, which is surrounded by beautiful countryside'. He was allowed one parcel from home, 'and soap, chocolate and home made cakes is all I really need'. These parcels, organised by the Red Cross, were very welcome, both in terms of morale and in providing items of clothing as well

as small luxuries. In January 1945 the *Leicester Advertiser* reported that Mr and Mrs David Lewin of West Street had received a letter from their son Leslie, also a prisoner of the Germans, to say that he was 'very well and had had some new clothes and boots' as well as 600 cigarettes from the Syston Red Cross 'rural pennies' fund.

POWs of the Germans were repatriated soon after VE Day. In June 1945 Lance Corporal Stanley Reast was welcomed back to Syston by 50 guests at a party at the Midland Hotel, arranged by his parents who lived in Central Avenue. A toast was drunk to the 'three musketeers', the others being Corporal Reg Preston, who had already returned home, and Private Teddy Black who was expected home soon after five years in a POW camp. The wait for news from the Far East, as well as the period before repatriation, were often much longer. Gunner Dennis Rowland Sharp went missing in Malaya in February 1942 after the fall of Singapore, and it was not until July 1944 that his mother received a postcard telling her that he was a prisoner of the Japanese in Taiwan. 'In his own writing', the *Leicester Advertiser* reported: 'Gunner Sharp says he is in good health, is working for pay' [sic]. In September 1945 he was able to send a telegram to her home in Tentercroft Avenue to say he was safe.

POWs in turn often had no news from home for long periods. Claude Evans, son of Mr and Mrs H.W. Evans of Sandford Road, was serving in the 6th Norfolk Regiment when he was captured by the Japanese after the fall of Singapore early in 1942. In the spring of 1945 he was rescued by American forces on the Philippine island of Luzon. In a letter to his parents from a hospital in the Philippines he wrote that he had received no news from home for the last 18 months; and how strange it felt 'to be free again, to eat civilised food and not to know hunger and want'. News of one of the earliest returns of a Far East POW to Syston - Private Sidney Sanders of the RAOC – appeared in the *Advertiser* in October 1945, when it also reported that 'with a friend [he] had the honour of hoisting the first British flag at Singapore after its liberation'.

THE PARISH OF SYSTON
LEICESTERSHIRE

REMEMBRANCE SUNDAY
7th November, 1948

UNVEILING & DEDICATION
OF
MEMORIAL PANELS
AT
THE WAR MEMORIAL

In memory of those who fell in the second World War, 1939—1945

Unveiling by : LORD HAZLERIGG
(Lord Lieutenant of Leicestershire)

Dedication by : Rev. F. B. TETLEY
(Vicar)

supported by

Rev. F. E. Lines, Rev E. H. Howard, Parish Council, British Legion, War Memorial Committee, Red Cross, N.F.S., R.A.O.B., Scouts, Constitutional Club, Working Men's Club, and the Town Cricket, Football and Bowling Clubs.

Programme for the unveiling and dedication of the Memorial Panels at the War Memorial – in memory of those who fell in the Second World War 1939-45.

ORDER OF SERVICE
AT
THE WAR MEMORIAL.

Hymn: "Lead Kindly Light."

Act of Homage: Mr. W. J. Prince.

Prayers: Rev. F. E. Lines.

Unveiling of Panels: Lord Hazlerigg.

Dedication of Panels: Rev. F. B. Tetley.
(VICAR)

Laying of Wreaths.

Scripture Reading: V. R. Pochin, Esq., J.P.

Last Post.

TWO MINUTES SILENCE.

Reveille.

Hymn: "O God our help in ages past."

BLESSING.

Organisations will assemble at the Park at 10 a.m., under the direction of Police Sergeant Shred, and will be ready to move off promptly at 10-15 a.m. The procession will march by way of Leicester Road to the War Memorial, headed by Syston Silver Band.

THE SYSTON PRESS, Printers, Melton Road, Syston

Hymn 1.

Lead, kindly Light, amid the encircling gloom,
    Lead Thou me on;
The night is dark, and I am far from home,
    Lead Thou me on.
Keep Thou my feet; I do not ask to see
The distant scene; one step enough for me.

I was not ever thus, nor pray'd that Thou
    Shouldst lead me on;
I loved to choose and see my path; but now
    Lead Thou me on.
I loved the garish day, and, spite of fears,
Pride ruled my will: remember not past years.

So long Thy power hath blest me, sure it still
    Will lead me on,
O'er moor and fen, o'er crag and torrent, till
    The night is gone.
And with the morn those Angel faces smile,
Which I have loved long since, and lost awhile.

Hymn 2.

O God, our help in ages past,
    Our hope for years to come,
Our shelter from the stormy blast,
    And our eternal home.

Beneath the shadow of Thy Throne
    Thy Saints have dwelt secure;
Sufficient is Thine Arm alone,
    And our defence is sure.

Before the hills in order stood,
    Or earth received her frame,
From everlasting Thou art God,
    To endless years the Same.

A thousand ages in Thy sight
    Are like an evening gone;
Short as the watch that ends the night
    Before the rising sun.

Time like an ever-rolling stream,
    Bears all its sons away;
They fly forgotten, as a dream
    Dies at the opening day.

O God, our help in ages past,
    Our hope for years to come,
Be Thou our guard while troubles last,
    And our eternal home.

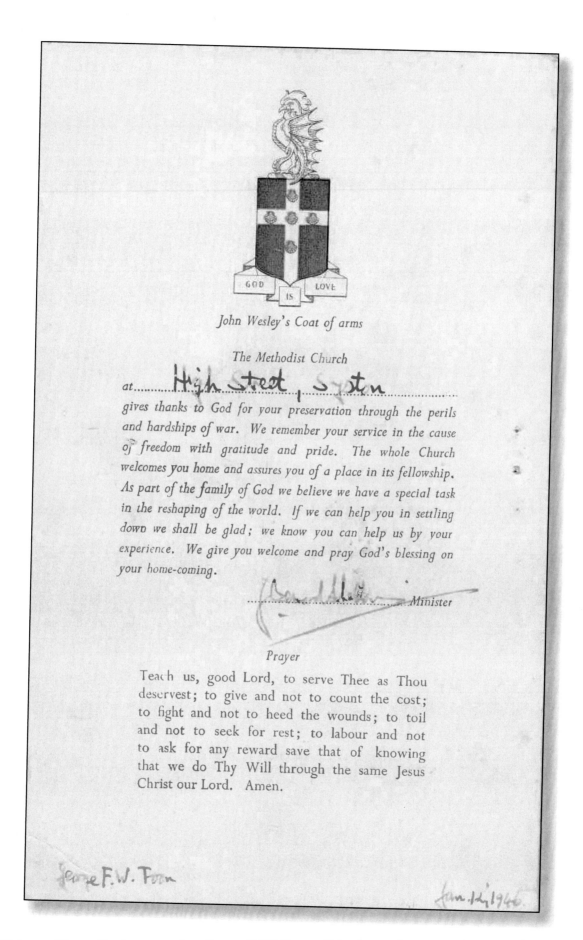

John Wesley's Coat of arms

The Methodist Church

at......*High Street, Syston*......

gives thanks to God for your preservation through the perils and hardships of war. We remember your service in the cause of freedom with gratitude and pride. The whole Church welcomes you home and assures you of a place in its fellowship. As part of the family of God we believe we have a special task in the reshaping of the world. If we can help you in settling down we shall be glad; we know you can help us by your experience. We give you welcome and pray God's blessing on your home-coming.

....................................Minister

Prayer

Teach us, good Lord, to serve Thee as Thou deservest; to give and not to count the cost; to fight and not to heed the wounds; to toil and not to seek for rest; to labour and not to ask for any reward save that of knowing that we do Thy Will through the same Jesus Christ our Lord. Amen.

George F. W. Toon

Jan. 14, 1946

A Welcome Home Card presented to George F. W. Toon of The Green, Syston, on his return from the war, by the High Street Methodist Church.

COMMEMORATED ON THE WORLD WAR II PANELS OF SYSTON WAR MEMORIAL

BAILEY, A.
BENTLEY, Bernard Harry
BENT, Matthew
BLACK, Sidney
BOLTON, Derrick Richard
BULL, Dor.
CARTER, S.
CHERRY, George Cecil
CLARKE, Frank
CLARKE, Victor William
CORBY, Edward Francis
CUNNINGTON, Cyril Frederick William
ENDWIG, Kenneth Jack
FERNSBY, Guy
FREER, William
GARLAND, Reginald Wyatt
GILBERT, Frederick Arthur
GOODWILL, William
GREGORY, Charles A.
GREGORY, Norman
HEGGS, Don
HEYWOOD, Peter
HILL, Dennis Frederick
HUNT, Joel Sarson
ILIFFE, William Harry
KNIGHT, A.
LEWIN, Charles Leonard Needham
NORTH, A.
OGDEN, Robert Arthur
ORCHARD, William
PAGE, Norman
QUINCEY, Thomas Arthur
SAICH, Eric William
SHORTER, Reginald
SQUIRES, Barbara Annie
TALBOTT, Walter Fergus
WALKER, George Alan
WARREN, William Frank
WESTBURY, William Norman
WHENHAM, John William Valentine
WHITTINGTON, Norman Colin
WILLDAY, John Henry
WRIGHT, Robert Andrew
YEATES, Jack

REMEMBERING THE FALLEN

Not everyone returned home safely, and discussions about how to commemorate Syston's World War II dead began even before the war ended. In April 1945 over 70 villagers attended a meeting of the Parish Council to consider some proposed options: to erect a memorial in Syston itself; 'to go with the county memorial'; or to do both. It was agreed to have a memorial in Syston, but the decision about what this should be was left 'for the boys when they come back'. A village hall or community centre was suggested, or a fund for the disabled and dependents of the fallen. The Syston and New Barkby War Memorial Committee, chaired by Ernest Quinn, was formed to raise the necessary money, and this was used to purchase 'Gandy's field' between West Street and the railway to establish the Memorial Playing Fields. New bronze panels were also added to the existing war memorial with the names of those who had died. These were unveiled in November 1948 by Lord Hazelrigg and dedicated by the vicar, Rev Tetley, following 'the largest procession for many years' between the park and the memorial. The memorial was located at that time in the centre of the village, at the junction of Barkby Road, High Street and Melton Road, and was moved to its current site in Central Park on Barkby Road in 1972.

10 LOOKING TO THE FUTURE – THE END OF WAR

The end of the war in Europe on Tuesday 8 May 1945 – VE Day – was celebrated in Syston with the same relief and thanksgiving as swept the rest of the country. The *Leicester Advertiser* reported on 12 May 1945 that:

'Flags in every street, decorated buildings, a victory peal on the church bells, thanksgiving services, children's street parties, bonfires, fireworks, dancing and singing in illuminated streets until the early hours of the morning, and a Victory Ball attended by 600 dancers, were highlights of Syston's VE celebrations'.

The celebrations in the park in St Peter's Street were particularly memorable for Jane Marshall, who was five at the time. She recalls being 'terrified of the fireworks and wanting to go home. I've never been keen on fireworks since then!'. The war memorial was decorated with Allied flags and 'the lion on top held a Union Jack in its mouth. Perhaps the old

thatched cottage in High Street, on which scores of miniature Union Jacks fluttered from the thatch-work, was the most picturesque of the decorated buildings'. An 'outsize' RAF flag was flown in St Peter's Street, 'pitted with bullet holes from a German plane when the flag was flying over an aerodrome. The residents were particularly proud of that one'; and the arrival of a brewer's dray outside 'a hostelry which was running short' was greeted with cheers from the customers.

On the following Saturday Victory celebrations were held on part of High Street, Bath Street, Lower Church Street, Brook Street and Turn Street, beginning with a tea on The Green followed by sports. There was dancing and community singing to a piano and piano-accordion accompaniment. Dorothy Foulds (nee Gilbert) also recalled that Postlethwaite's off licence on the corner of Brookfield Street had a piano, and 'the man played for the event. He'd keep playing as long as there

VE Day – Gamble's cottage on High Street decorated with Union Flags. *(Ray Young)*

was a glass of beer on the piano'. Jennifer Turner, who attended the VE celebration on The Green, recalls that:

'High Street was very quiet then. No cars were allowed except for doctors' cars. Delivery vans mainly mornings only. The minimal amount of buses could be diverted for this occasion. There was dancing at night but I did not partake in that as I was too young. Even the bonfire was there on The Green, (which was cobbled then). Obviously the older teenagers had more fun but we had a party with sandwiches, jellies and cakes. One of the young men arrived on a large motor bike, I remember all the girls crowding round him. There was a bonfire (it was not as enormous as they build them now), and they burnt an effigy of Hitler and also some fireworks were let off. This was repeated on VJ day, but Dad was back then so we celebrated in Leicester with some of his AFS friend's families'.

An iced cake was taken to the Leicester Royal Infirmary, for patients in the Frome Ward 'where Miss Mary Payne of The Green was one of the patients', and more street parties were held in different parts of Syston in the following days. One local woman who was nine at the end of the war recalled that 'We had a street party for the children in the Meadway for VE Day (a long trestle table with food contributed by the mothers) and we had a party in the farmyard of Graham's farm [Roundhill Farm on Barkby Lane] for VJ day, possibly also with games. VE Day meant more to us children I think'.

Not everyone was able to rejoice on these occasions. Many people in Syston had lost loved ones during the war, but the family of George Cecil Cherry, who lived in Mostyn Avenue, received the news that everyone dreaded on VE Day itself. 'There was a street party organised for Mostyn Avenue', his daughter Joan recalled: 'the tables extended half way down the street and there were flags from one side to the other. Unfortunately that was the day we received the telegram that told us Dad had been killed in action, so my Mum wouldn't allow us to attend the party'. Even though her own story had a happy ending, VE Day was also very hard for Mary Gamble, whose husband Ernest did not return from the war until March 1947. There was an impromptu party in the road, she recalled:

'People brought out food and drinks and somebody brought out their (wind-up) gramophone and all the local people were dancing in the street. But I couldn't celebrate because my husband was still fighting the war against the Japanese in the Far East. I didn't

VE Day – the street party in Tentercroft Avenue looking down towards Melton Road.

know if he was safe, or when he might come home. I went into the house and cried'.

Around 600 serving men and women had yet to return to Syston in June 1945, according to a *Leicester Advertiser* report of a meeting 'filled with parishioners' at the Adult School to discuss a war memorial. In July, however, 'hundreds of villagers' took advantage of the peace to have a holiday by the seaside, Skegness and Scarborough reportedly being the most popular venues.

More street parties were held to celebrate VJ Day in August 1945, but they were relatively low key by comparison with VE Day. There was also a concert by the Wigston Temperance Band, followed by an evening cricket match between 'ladies and gentlemen', a Whist Drive and dances. The bells of St Peter's were rung for a united service of thanksgiving attended by over 300 villagers. Hymns were sung by a united choir, and Miss Muriel Toon sang 'Land of Hope and Glory'. This was probably the service recalled by Vivienne Everitt at which: 'Everyone's name in the village who had been involved in the conflict were read out. It was a happy time but also very sad; there was a lot of crying and some people passed out'.

The first new post-war housing in Syston was completed in the summer of 1945 and consisted of a bungalow built for Mr Carnell of School Lane on the same site as the demolished cottage in which his parents had lived for 55 years. In the meantime, Barrow Rural District Council (RDC) had begun to address the demand for new housing once wartime building restrictions were lifted. 'When our men come back from the Forces they would want houses, and quickly', as Ernest Quinn, Chairman of the Parish Council said in April 1945. A site for the first new houses was selected at the back of the 'Avenues', and in May that year the RDC allocated 100 temporary houses to be built at Syston, Sileby and Birstall, with priority to the first two. Applicants were recommended to the RDC by the Parish Council on a 'points' basis according to need, but it was a very slow process: 'something like a game of snakes and ladders', as the Chairman of the RDC's Housing Committee described it in December 1945: 'without the ladders'. The 'prefabs',

on Gloucester Avenue, were completed in 1947.

There were difficult adjustments to be made in the post-war period as the country faced serious financial problems along with the massive task of reconstruction: but despite the continuing rationing of food and other goods and the absence of loved ones still waiting to be released from the Forces, 1945 ended on a note of optimism. On 24 December the *Leicester Mercury* reported 'Leicester's Biggest Wedding Rush Since 1939' - the registrar said he had been 'impressed by the spirit of happiness, the like of which he had never witnessed during the war' – and the streets of the city were crowded with Christmas shoppers. 'Grown-up people', the *Mercury* continued:

'will find it not easy at this season to keep clear of the reflection that this is not their first experience of Christmas peace celebrations following hard on years of war… [but] the spirit of Christmas persists, glorying in the victories won by the forces of good over evil, renewing all the hope that derives from the Christian meaning of life and man's purpose in it. Surely the Christmas message never fell upon a world that more sorely needed its comfort and its hope… the Happy Christmas of 1945 will mark the dawn of a new era of peace on earth'.

VE Day – the street party in Barkby Road.

SOURCES FOR THE BOOK

Much of this book is based on memories of Syston during the Second World War, passed on in writing, face-to-face interviews or by telephone. Photographs, written memoirs and other documents have also been made available to the authors.

We have also drawn on the following documentary sources:

Books and pamphlets

Auster Quarterly, Vol 1, No 1 (Spring 1975)

Eatough's Ltd. Commemoration Souvenir (1945)

Bonser R., *Aviation in Leicestershire and Rutland* (Midland Publishing, 2001)

Gregory C., *Syston as I Remember It: memories of the Syston area in Leicestershire by local people who lived and worked there*, (Leicestershire Libraries and Information Service, 1992)

Hitchman A. & Preston M., *The History of the Auster Aeroplane* (International Auster Heritage Group, 3rd revised edition, 2006)

Lewis F. & Young R., *Syston Methodist Church: centenary souvenir booklet* (Clipper Print, 1991)

Newspapers

Newspapers have been an invaluable source of information, particularly the *Leicester Mercury* and the *Leicester Advertiser*, a weekly publication with a page of news from the Melton area, including Syston. The *Melton Mowbray Times and Vale of Belvoir Gazette* also published a Syston edition, the *Syston and District* Times, but very few copies of this have survived. Fortunately, one that did - a December 1941 edition - included a chronology of events for that year.

Other documentary sources

Barkby Pochin School Log Book 1914 – 1982 (Record Office for Leicestershire, Leicester & Rutland (subsequently ROLLR), DE8776/1

Cossington C of E School Log Book 1936 – 1976 (ROLLR, E/LB/79/2)

Kelly's Directory of Leicestershire & Rutland, 1936; 1941

New Barkby Women's Institute Minute Books (1938 – 44)

Queniborough National School Log Book 1923 – 1946 (ROLLR, E/LB/257/3)

Syston Men's Adult School, *Minutes* 1929 – 1965 (ROLLR, E/MB/B/320/1-3)

Syston *Parish Magazine* (1939 – 41)

Syston Parochial Schools, Managers' Minutes 1903 – 1946 (Record Office for Leicestershire, Leicester & Rutland (ROLLR), DE4498/88

Websites

Ancestry - Census and migration records (www.ancestry.com)

BBC People's War – an online archive of memories and images contributed to the BBC between June 2003 and January 2006 (www.bbc.co.uk/history/ww2peopleswar/)

Commonwealth War Graves Commission (CWGC) – information about Syston men buried or commemorated in CWGC cemeteries, or commemorated on its memorials – www.cwgc.org

Leicestershire War memorials – information about those named on the Syston War Memorial - www.leicestershirewarmemorials.co.uk/war/memorials/view/1121